EIGHT LIGHTS
A Hanukkah Devotional for Followers of Yeshua

DARREN N. HUCKEY

Eight Lights: A Hanukkah Devotional for Followers of Yeshua
Copyright © 2013 Darren Huckey. All rights reserved.
Publication rights Emet HaTorah.

Publisher grants permission to reference short quotations (fewer than 400 words) in reviews, magazines, newspapers, web sites, or other publications. Requests for permission to reproduce more than 400 words can be made at:

www.emethatorah.com/contact

Scriptural quotations are from The Holy Bible, English Standard Version, copyright © 2001 by Crossway Bibles, a division of Good News Publishers. Used by permission. All rights reserved.

Cover Design: Darren Huckey

Emet HaTorah
PO Box 28281, Macon, GA 31221-8281 USA
www.emethatorah.com

Comments and questions: www.emethatorah.com/contact

Darren N. Huckey

Eight Lights

A Hanukkah Devotional for Followers of Yeshua

"*I am the light of the world.
Whoever follows me will not walk in darkness,
but will have the light of life.*"

~ *Jesus, John 8:12* ~

Contents

Discover (Introduction to Hanukkah) 9

Celebrate (How to Celebrate Hanukkah) 16

Reflect (Devotionals for the Eight Nights) 21

    Night One 21

    Night Two 25

    Night Three 29

    Night Four 33

    Night Five 37

    Night Six 41

    Night Seven 45

    Night Eight 51

Remember (1 Maccabees) 55

CHAPTER ONE
Discover

An Introduction to Hanukkah

Do you believe in miracles? The chorus of a popular Hanukkah song asks this question. Why? Because Hanukkah is a remembrance and celebration of miracles. They are miracles that were done on behalf of the Jewish nation more than two thousand years ago. But why do we celebrate these miracles every year even after two thousand years? Because the Almighty knows that humans are a selectively forgetful people. We tend to forget the kindnesses that were lavished on us, while clinging to the hurts and the pains inflicted on us by others. Therefore, we need a cycle of reminders to bring to the forefront of our lives the goodness that the Merciful One has shown us. We celebrate each of the biblical festivals as a reminder of Who God is, what He has done for us and what He will do in the future.

Although Hanukkah—instituted a few hundred years prior to the New Testament period—is technically not one of the biblical holy days, we can learn a great deal about our faith, our Creator and our Messiah from this yearly festival. Tonight we begin an eight day remembrance of the redemption of Israel through the hand of the Maccabees, servants of the God of Israel, in the days just prior to the coming of our Master. There is a lesson to be learned from the lights of each night of Hanukkah. May our ears hear and our hearts be awakened to the lessons of these Eight Lights.

WHAT IS HANUKKAH?

Let's get this straight from the beginning: Hanukkah is not the Jewish version of Christmas. In fact, the celebration of Hanukkah precedes the institution of Christmas by several hundred years. Nevertheless, Hanukkah has increasingly been commercialized and exploited by materialistic elements of Western culture in a way very similar to that of Christmas. This, however, is the extent of the commonalities between the two holidays. Hanukkah is the yearly celebration that remembers God's redemption of Israel from the hand of her pagan oppressors. In a nutshell, the story of Hanukkah goes like this ...

Nearly two hundred years before the time of our Master, the Syrian-Greek armies invaded and plundered Israel, particularly the Holy Temple in Jerusalem. They ransacked the Temple and converted it into a pagan temple for their god, Zeus. Following on the heels of this event, the practice of Judaism was outlawed and the Jews were forbidden to participate in their religion in any way. They were forced to forsake the covenant God had made with them and to assimilate into Greek culture. What did this mean? They were no longer able to read and study the Torah. They were forbidden to observe the Holy Sabbath or celebrate the biblical feasts. They were forbidden to circumcise their children (on pain of death). They were forced to eat swine and to offer sacrifices to the idols of pagan gods. The Greeks would not tolerate a people who had any semblance of holiness. The Jews were forced to look like, act like and worship like the rest of the nations around them.

Eventually, a priestly family (the Hasmoneans)—initiated by their father, Mathathias—rose up against their oppressors because of their zeal to keep the covenant of the Lord. Eventually Mathathias passed away, leaving his son Judah (or Judas) to lead the resistance. Judah became a mighty military commander who waged a fierce war on the pagan armies. He relied upon the mercies of God for his military strength and humbly led his small armies to victory against the powerful Greek armies who often outnumbered them ten to one or greater.

After pushing out the Greeks from Judea, Judah led the people in the enormous project of restoring the Holy Temple, which culminated in a rededication of the Holy House on the twenty-fifth of the Hebrew month of Kislev. This dedication ceremony lasted eight days:

> And they kept the dedication of the altar eight days, and they offered burnt offerings with joy, and sacrifices of salvation, and of praise ...
> (1 Maccabees 4:56)

From that time forward, beginning on the anniversary of the rededication, the Israelites resolved to observe yearly an eight day feast in memorial of this event:

> And Judah, and his brethren, and all the church of Israel decreed, that the day of the dedication of the altar should be kept in its season from year to year for eight days, from the five and twentieth day of the month of Kislev, with joy and gladness. (1 Maccabees 4:59)

This is where we get the word Hanukkah. Hanukkah means "dedication." Hanukkah is also known as the Feast of Dedication and the Festival of Lights, which are the main themes that permeate the Hanukkah story. God delivered the Israelites out of the hand of their oppressors in a miraculous way, and Hanukkah is a yearly reminder of the miracle of that deliverance.

There is another miracle associated with Hanukkah that is not recorded in the book of Maccabees. According to the Talmud (b.*Shabbat* 21b), when the priests went to kindle the lights of the Temple menorah, only one small flask of oil was found. Even though it was enough to last only one day, they decided to use it. Miraculously, it lasted eight days ... long enough for new, Temple-grade, pure olive oil to be made.

Hanukkah is a time to remember everything that makes God's people unique, holy, and distinct from the world. It is a time to shake ourselves from our slumber and the comfortable trappings of assimilation. Hanukkah is a time to say no to the world and yes to our Heavenly Father. Hanukkah is a time to shine forth the light of our Messiah.

Yeshua and Hanukkah

Followers of Yeshua know him as the Light of the World. John says, "In him was life, and the life was the light of men. The light shines in the darkness, and the darkness has not overcome it" (John 1:4–5). He also says that he was "the true light, which gives light to everyone" (John 1:9). Yeshua says something similar about himself as well. He says, "I am the light of the world. Whoever follows me will not walk in darkness, but will have the light of life" (John 8:12). He is not hesitant to share the fact that he is the beacon of the Father's light shining brightly into this world.

Several years prior to these events, when Simeon the priest saw Yeshua as an infant in the Temple, he called him "a light for revelation to the Gentiles, and for glory to your people Israel" (Luke 2:32). Simeon recognized the penetrating light contained within the person of Yeshua, which would expose the darkness of the world. As Yeshua has said, "For nothing is hidden that will not be made manifest, nor is anything secret that will not be known and come to light" (Luke 8:17).

At the Transfiguration, Matthew records that Yeshua's "face shone like the sun, and his clothes became white as light" (Matthew 17:2). This alludes back to Moses receiving the Torah at Sinai and the radiance of the Almighty illuminating his face (Exodus 34:29–35). Yeshua's divine encounter reflected Moses's encounter in order to show his disciples his affinity with his Father. Just as Moses was the First Redeemer, Yeshua was the Second Redeemer who shone with the brilliance of his Father. Hanukkah is the perfect time to remember our Master, "the true light, which gives light to everyone."

The thematic connections of Yeshua with Hanukkah are obvious. But what about any direct connections? Did Yeshua celebrate Hanukkah? Is there any way we can know this for certain? We need to take a look at an event in the Gospel of John to find out. However, first we need to know some background information to help us understand the context of what is happening.

The Torah prescribes Jewish males to travel to Jerusalem for the three major pilgrimage festivals of *Pesach* (Passover), *Shavuot* (Pentecost) and *Sukkot* (Tabernacles). The commandment for these feasts to be kept as pilgrimage festivals is found in Exodus 23:14-17, where it begins, "Three times in the year you shall keep a feast to me …" It then describes each of these three feasts and concludes, "Three times in the year shall all your males appear before the LORD God."

Although these are the "big three" that Scripture mandates all Jewish males make pilgrimage to attend, Hanukkah is not even mentioned in the Hebrew Scriptures, the "Old Testament." Yet we read of it in the Apostolic Scriptures (the "New Testament"). John tells us, "At that time the Feast of Dedication took place at Jerusalem. It was winter, and Jesus was walking in the temple, in the colonnade of Solomon" (John 10:22–23).

As stated previously, Hanukkah means "dedication." This festival is called the Feast of Dedication because it commemorates the rededication of the Holy Temple after it was defiled by pagan idolaters. John makes it a point to record that Yeshua traveled up to Jerusalem from his home in the Galilee in order to observe the feast of Hanukkah as he did the pilgrimage festivals. Why then was it so important that Yeshua travel from the Galilee up to Jerusalem to be at the Temple for Hanukkah? Because Hanukkah, remember, commemorates the rededication of the Temple ... the rededication of his Father's House. Yeshua knew a time was coming when His Father's house would once again lay desolate. But the next time, rather than just a few years, the Temple would remain in ruins for over two thousand years. To him this was nearly unbearable. He walked the courtyards of the Holy Temple to remind his brothers and sisters of the reason for its previous destruction and to warn them about its imminent demise. He called them to repentance in order to try to reverse the impending judgment. Hanukkah was the perfect time to do this, because of the themes of rededication fresh on people's minds. The people approached him and asked, "How long will you keep us in suspense? If you are the Christ, tell us plainly." He replied in this manner:

> I told you, and you do not believe. The works that I do in my Father's name bear witness about me, but you do not believe because you are not among my sheep. My sheep hear my voice, and I know them, and they follow me. I give them eternal life, and they will never perish, and no one will snatch them out of my hand. My Father, who has given them to me, is greater than all, and no one is able to snatch them out of the Father's hand. I and the Father are one. (John 10:24–30)

He tells the people that his works not only attest not only to his claim to be the Messiah, but also to his sonship. His works verify his identity. Yeshua reminds his followers that their works also attest to their identity:

> "You are the salt of the earth, but if salt has lost its taste, how shall its saltiness be restored? It is no longer good for anything except to

be thrown out and trampled under people's feet. You are the light of the world. A city set on a hill cannot be hidden. Nor do people light a lamp and put it under a basket, but on a stand, and it gives light to all in the house. In the same way, let your light shine before others, so that they may see your good works and give glory to your Father who is in heaven." (Matthew 5:13–16)

During the first century, many of the Jewish people had lost both their light and their saltiness. They had forgotten who they were supposed to be. They offered no flavor, nor did their light shine forth into the darkness. Yeshua challenged those who came after him to take up their commission to be light and salt. The challenge still goes forth today. As followers of Yeshua, Hanukkah's central theme of light is extremely relevant to our purpose of remembering both the Master—the True Light—and our responsibility to reflect his light to a darkened world, devoid of purpose and hope. Let's take up that call to be light and salt and reflect our Master through our deeds and not just our speech.

CHAPTER TWO

Celebrate

The Basics of Celebrating Hanukkah

Hanukkah Traditions

There are many Hanukkah traditions we will not explore in detail here, but I would like you to at least be aware of them. First, since the tradition of Hanukkah revolves around the miracle of the oil in the Temple menorah lasting for eight days, fried foods are the choice for the holiday. The two primary ones are *latkes* (potato pancakes) and *sufganiyot* (jelly-filled doughnuts). The internet is full of recipes for these items, offering a wide variety of choices for how they are made.

Next, there are *dreidels*. A dreidel is a four-sided, spinning top that has one Hebrew letter on each side. It is usually played with chocolate *gelt* (chocolate wrapped to look like gold coins). At the beginning of a round, each player puts in some of their gelt and one player spins. The letter the dreidel lands on determines the action of the player. He will either put more gelt in, take some (or all) of it out, or simply pass the play to the next person. Dreidels can be purchased inexpensively online or at a Judaica shop. Again, a quick internet search will pull up the full instructions on playing.

And like any other festival, there is always singing, dancing and joy. Traditional songs include "Maoz Tzur" ("Rock of Ages"), "Oh, Hanukkah! Oh, Hanukkah!" and the "Dreidel Song." At the end of this section we have included the lyrics to a Messianic song called "Ohr Olam" ("Light of the World"), written by Troy Mitchell, based on Yeshua's teaching in Matthew chapter five. We have also included a website address where you can actually hear the song to learn the melody or play it at your Hanukkah celebration.

The focal point of each evening is the lighting of the Hanukkah menorah, called a *hanukkiah*. This is a small menorah that differs from the Temple menorah in that it has nine candlesticks rather than seven. There are eight for the eight nights of Hanukkah, and an extra one called the *shamash*, the servant candle, which is used to light the other candles. The candles are generally small and burn for only a few hours. Each night additional candles are lit until the last night when all eight candles (and the shamash) are burning. Specific instructions on lighting the hanukkiah are in the next section below. You will need a total of forty-four candles for the entire week. These are sold in sets and are generally inexpensive to purchase.

Last, but definitely not the least, it is tradition on any holy day to give *tzedakah*—charity (explained more on night seven)—to those who have need. The Almighty says we are not to come before Him empty-handed (Exodus 23:15; 34:20; Deuteronomy 16:16). This is a reminder in our day to open our hands to those in need. This can be done in a number of ways and is entirely at your discretion.

Lighting the Hanukkiah

Lighting the hanukkiah is simple, but can be confusing the first time or two. There are a couple of rules to guide us through lighting the hanukkiah. The first is the adding of candles. During the years just prior to the time of Yeshua's earthly life, the sages ruled that the number of candles should be increased each night, rather than decreased, just as our joy should increase during the festival and not decrease. Therefore, at the onset of each night, a new shamash and an additional candle is added to the number of candles used the previous night. The candles are placed beginning from right to left with the front of the hanukkiah facing you.

On the first night, we place the shamash and then a single candle that represents the first night. On the second night, we place the shamash and then two candles that represent the second night. On the third night, we place the shamash and then three candles that represent the third night, etc.

The procedure for lighting the candles is to first light the shamash and then use it to light the other candles. Remember, the shamash is used only to "serve" by lighting the other candles. It does not count as one of the eight Hanukkah lights for the evening. From there the candles are lit from left to right, starting with the newest candle.

Traditionally, a blessing is said before lighting the candles. We have included these blessings here. Please note, we have included an alternate version of the second blessing that is more applicable to non-Jewish participants.

The following are traditional Jewish blessings with an alternative to include non-Jewish participation.

Blessing for Kindling the Candles

After the shamash is lit, continue to hold the shamash and say the following blessings. This blessing may be omitted for those of us who are not Jewish.

בָּרוּךְ אַתָּה יְיָ אֱלֹהֵינוּ מֶלֶךְ הָעוֹלָם אֲשֶׁר קִדְּשָׁנוּ בְּמִצְוֹתָיו, וְצִוָּנוּ לְהַדְלִיק נֵר שֶׁל חֲנֻכָּה.

Baruch Atah Adonai Eloheinu Melech HaOlam, asher kidshanu b'mitzvotav v'tzivanu l'hadlik ner shel Hanukkah.

Blessed are You, O Lord Our God, King of the Universe, Who has sanctified us with Your commandments and commanded us to kindle the lights of Hanukkah.

Second Blessing

בָּרוּךְ אַתָּה יְיָ אֱלֹהֵינוּ מֶלֶךְ הָעוֹלָם שֶׁעָשָׂה נִסִּים לַאֲבוֹתֵינוּ בַּיָּמִים הָהֵם בַּזְּמַן הַזֶּה.

Baruch Atah Adonai Eloheinu Melech HaOlam, she'asah nisim l'avoteinu, b'yamim haheim bazman hazeh.

Blessed are You, O Lord our God, King of the Universe, Who made miracles for our forefathers in those days at this time.

THOSE OF US WHO ARE NOT JEWISH SHOULD CONSIDER USING THE FOLLOWING BLESSING:

בָּרוּךְ אַתָּה יְיָ אֱלֹהֵינוּ מֶלֶךְ הָעוֹלָם שֶׁעָשָׂה נִסִּים לִבְנֵי יִשְׂרָאֵל בַּיָּמִים הָהֵם בַּזְּמַן הַזֶּה.

Baruch Atah Adonai Eloheinu Melech HaOlam, she'asah nisim livnei Yisrael, b'yamim haheim bazman hazeh.

Blessed are You, O Lord our God, King of the Universe, Who made miracles for the Children of Israel in those days at this time.

THIRD BLESSING

THE FOLLOWING BLESSING IS RECITED ONLY ON THE FIRST NIGHT OF HANUKKAH:

בָּרוּךְ אַתָּה יְיָ אֱלֹהֵינוּ מֶלֶךְ הָעוֹלָם שֶׁהֶחֱיָנוּ וְקִיְּמָנוּ וְהִגִּיעָנוּ לַזְּמַן הַזֶּה.

Baruch Atah Adonai Eloheinu Melech HaOlam, shehecheyanu, v'kiyamanu vehigianu lazman hazeh.

Blessed are You, O Lord Our God, King of the Universe, Who has kept us alive, sustained us and brought us to this season.

Below is a song by Troy Mitchell that takes the teaching of Yeshua in Matthew 5:14–16 and ties it to Proverbs 6:23, which says, "For the commandment is a lamp and the Torah a light." The word *mitzvah* means commandment. By living out the Word of God, we become lamps that shine the light of Torah and Yeshua (the Torah-Made-Flesh) into the darkness. If you would like to learn the melody for this song and use it during your Hanukkah celebrations, you can hear it at **http://emethatorah.com/ohr-olam**.

OHR OLAM

You are the light of the world
Let your light shine before all men
That they may see your deeds
And glorify our Father in Heaven

The lamp is the mitzvah
The light it shines is the Torah
The lamp is the mitzvah
The light it shines is the Torah

"Ohr Olam" words and music by Troy Mitchell.
© 2005 by Troy Mitchell. All Rights Reserved.
Printed with permission.

CHAPTER THREE
Reflect

Devotionals for Each Night of Hanukkah

Night One
AVODAH

Now the days drew near that Mattathias should die, and he said to his sons: "Now has pride and chastisement gotten strength, and the time of destruction, and the wrath of indignation. Now therefore, O my sons, be zealous for the Torah, and give your lives for the covenant of your fathers. And call to remembrance the works of the fathers, which they have done in their generations" (1 Maccabees 2:49-51).

The very first night of Hanukkah! One small candle burns in solitude, a single flame in the darkness. Well, sort of. This is the first night of Hanukkah where we light the first candle! But how many candles do you see? Do you see one, or do you see two?

That second candle that's hiding in the back (or off to the side, depending on your hanukkiah) is a special candle. It's called a *shamash*, or servant. Its job is to pass the flame to each of the eight candles of the Hanukkah menorah. Its job is to serve (*avodah*) the other candles by passing its light and heat to them. It doesn't get counted like the other candles, yet it is always present. Every night we first light the *shamash* and then use it to light the other candles. It really has a thankless job. The shamash works hard to make the other candles shine brightly, but receives little attention for this important task and is not counted among the special Eight Lights of Hanukkah.

In John 13, Yeshua is with his disciples preparing to eat what would be his last earthly meal before his death, burial and resurrection. In that very last meal Yeshua reveals the most important thing he wants to leave to his disciples. Was it a secret teaching? A precious jewel? A map to buried treasures? No. It was an example of serving others. Just when his disciples thought that one of the servants of the house would come and wash the scum off of their nasty feet, Yeshua took a hold of the water basin, grabbed a towel and bent down to wash their feet.

Peter nearly fainted. As a matter of fact, he refused to have Yeshua wash his feet. He thought it was indignant and unbecoming of his great rabbi—the greatest rabbi to walk the face of the earth!—to wash the nasty feet of others, especially his own. If anything, shouldn't he be the one washing Yeshua's feet, and not the reverse? But Yeshua rebuked Peter for thinking this way. He told him of the absolute necessity of serving them. Yeshua explained to him very clearly the significance of what he was doing:

> When he had washed their feet and put on his outer garments and resumed his place, he said to them, "Do you understand what I have done to you? You call me Teacher and Lord, and you are right, for so I am. If I then, your Lord and Teacher, have washed your feet, you also ought to wash one another's feet. For I have given you an example, that you also should do just as I have done to you. Truly, truly, I say to you, a servant is not greater than his master, nor is a messenger greater than the one who sent him. (John 13:12-16)

He set the model for how to serve others by serving them himself. If we consider the subject, the words Yeshua spoke in John 13 overlap his words in Luke 6 and can be combined to convey a single statement:

> Truly, truly, I say to you, a servant is not greater than his master, nor is a messenger greater than the one who sent him. A disciple is not above his teacher, but everyone when he is fully trained will be like his teacher. (John 13:16; Luke 6:40)

Yeshua expects his followers to imitate him, so serving others should be at the top of our list. These words echoed in Simon Peter's memory, and he carried them with him to his death. You see, a little while earlier, a few of the disciples had argued over who was the greatest. (Surely not Peter, right?) Yeshua responded in much the same way as he did the night he washed their feet. He told them, "But whoever would be great among you must be your servant, and whoever would be first among you must be your slave" (Matthew 20:26b-27). Yeshua placed the utmost importance on serving others. In fact, he concluded his rebuke by saying it was indeed his very mission: "The Son of Man came not to be served but to serve, and to give his life as a ransom for many" (Matthew 20:28).

As disciples of Yeshua, serving others should be in our nature. But we should serve like the shamash, without waiting for a "thank you" or expecting any kind of reward. Our Master taught us in this regard:

> Will any one of you who has a servant plowing or keeping sheep say to him when he has come in from the field, "Come at once and recline at table"? Will he not rather say to him, "Prepare supper for me, and dress properly, and serve me while I eat and drink, and afterward you will eat and drink"? Does he thank the servant because he did what was commanded? So you also, when you have done all that you were commanded, say, "We are unworthy servants; we have only done what was our duty." (Luke 17:7-10)

You see, it all begins with the single flame of the Shamash, the Servant. Yeshua lived the life of a servant. He is called the Suffering Servant. He is the Shamash. By serving his disciples, Yeshua lit a flame in them that would burn in their hearts for the rest of their lives, driving them to return that example by serving others. Just as Yeshua was the shamash and served his disciples, so may we also carry the light of our service into the darkness so the light of Yeshua may shine brightly in this world.

DISCUSSION

1. What's the most important candle of Hanukkah and why?

2. How did Yeshua exemplify the shamash?

3. Why did Peter argue with Yeshua over having his feet washed?

4. How did Peter begin to serve others after Yeshua's example?

5. How have others served you lately?

6. How have you served others lately?

7. What was your attitude in serving others?

Night Two

AHAVAH

And they said every man to his neighbor: "Let us raise up the low condition of our people, and let us fight for our people, and our sanctuary." (1 Maccabees 3:43)

The second night of Hanukkah! Two candles (plus the shamash) are burning brightly in our hanukkiahs, eager to teach us a lesson for our souls. What do they have to teach us? Let us learn the lesson of the Two Lights.

One time, a very learned Torah scholar approached Yeshua and asked, "Which commandment is the most important of all?" Yeshua responded in the following manner:

> The most important is, "Hear, O Israel: The Lord our God, the Lord is one. And you shall love the Lord your God with all your heart and with all your soul and with all your mind and with all your strength." (Mark 12:29-30)

But he didn't just stop there. He continued by adding, *The second is this: "You shall love your neighbor as yourself." There is no other commandment greater than these.* (Mark 12:31).

Yeshua says there is not just one great commandment, but two, upon which "depend all the Law and the Prophets" (Matthew 22:40). Our two candles on this second night of Hanukkah remind us of *ahavah*—love. They remind us of the love Yeshua expects of us. These two flames burning in front of us tonight are here to remind us of the flames that should burn within our hearts: love for our Heavenly Father and love for our neighbor.

Yeshua makes it clear that love is the greatest commandment and highest calling we can ever live up to. He says that the proper fulfillment of all of the commandments is dependent upon love. In another account of the scholar asking him this all-important question, Yeshua concludes by commissioning the scholar, "Do this, and you will live." Most people think of love as a feeling, emotion or an inner resolve. But Yeshua says, "Do this." How is love done? What does love look like? This is what the scholar wanted to know. Wasn't "feeling" love enough?

Like a good rabbi, Yeshua doesn't leave us guessing. He gives a parable to illustrate the practical application of what he is speaking about. He explains what "loving your neighbor" is all about. You may have heard of it. It's called the Parable of the Good Samaritan. It goes like this:

> A man was going down from Jerusalem to Jericho, and he fell among robbers, who stripped him and beat him and departed, leaving him half dead. Now by chance a priest was going down that road, and when he saw him he passed by on the other side. So likewise a Levite, when he came to the place and saw him, passed by on the other side. But a Samaritan, as he journeyed, came to where he was, and when he saw him, he had compassion. He went to him and bound up his wounds, pouring on oil and wine. Then he set him on his own animal and brought him to an inn and took care of him. And the next day he took out two denarii and gave them to the innkeeper, saying, "Take care of him, and whatever more you spend, I will repay you when I come back." (Luke 10:30-35)

At the end of the parable, Yeshua asks the scholar, *"Which of these three, do you think, proved to be a neighbor to the man who fell among the robbers?" He said, "The one who showed him mercy." And Jesus said to him, "You go, and do likewise"* (verses 36–37). Love is active. It is not based on emotions or feelings, but on a desire for the welfare of another. We "do" the commandments because of our love for our Heavenly Father (or at least we should). We "do" mitzvot to help others because of our love for them and our concern for their needs.

In the famous Chapter of Love (1 Corinthians 13), the apostle Paul describes love in detailed terms, showing that it is supreme above anything we could give back to God:

If I speak in the tongues of men and of angels, but have not love, I am a noisy gong or a clanging cymbal. And if I have prophetic powers, and understand all mysteries and all knowledge, and if I have all faith, so as to remove mountains, but have not love, I am nothing. If I give away all I have, and if I deliver up my body to be burned, but have not love, I gain nothing.

Love is patient and kind; love does not envy or boast; it is not arrogant or rude. It does not insist on its own way; it is not irritable or resentful; it does not rejoice at wrongdoing, but rejoices with the truth. Love bears all things, believes all things, hopes all things, endures all things.

Love never ends. As for prophecies, they will pass away; as for tongues, they will cease; as for knowledge, it will pass away. For we know in part and we prophesy in part, but when the perfect comes, the partial will pass away. When I was a child, I spoke like a child, I thought like a child, I reasoned like a child. When I became a man, I gave up childish ways. For now we see in a mirror dimly, but then face to face. Now I know in part; then I shall know fully, even as I have been fully known.

So now faith, hope, and love abide, these three; but the greatest of these is love.

John, the apostle whom Yeshua loved, wrote instructions for us as well:

For this is the message that you have heard from the beginning, that we should love one another ... By this we know love, that he laid down his life for us, and we ought to lay down our lives for the brothers. But if anyone has the world's goods and sees his brother in need, yet closes his heart against him, how does God's love abide in him? Little children, let us not love in word or talk but in deed and in truth. (1 John 3:11,16-18)

The Maccabees showed their love for both the Almighty and their neighbor by fighting for "our people, and our sanctuary" (1 Maccabees 3:43). They fought to preserve the lives of their kinsmen and preserve the honor of God. Their love was not only in word, but also in deed. May we take the lesson of these Two Lights and carry the love of Yeshua into this dark world.

Discussion

1. What commandments do the Two Candles remind us of?

2. Can you describe what love is?

3. What parable does Yeshua tell to teach us about love?

4. What lesson can we learn from the parable of the Good Samaritan?

5. What does John say true love looks like?

6. How did the Maccabees display their love?

7. What are some practical ways we can display our love to others?

Night Three
TEFILLAH

"You, O Lord, have chosen this house for your name to be called upon therein, that it might be a house of prayer and supplication for your people. Be avenged of this man, and his army, and let them fall by the sword. Remember their blasphemies and suffer them not to continue any longer." (1 Maccabees 7:37–38)

Tonight is the third night of Hanukkah! See the flicker of the flames? Feel their warmth as you approach them? Three candles (and the shamash) work together to bring us light and joy. But what lesson do these three candles bring us? What can they teach us on this, the third night of Hanukkah? These Three Lights shine brightly tonight to remind us of the three times of our day that we are to seek the face of the Holy One. They remind us of our responsibility of *tefillah*, or prayer.

These are the designated times of prayer: *Shacharit* (Morning), *Minchah* (Afternoon) and *Maariv* (Evening). We see an example of this pattern of prayer in the book of Daniel:

> He got down on his knees three times a day and prayed and gave thanks before his God, as he had done previously. (Daniel 6:10)

According to Jewish tradition, Abraham instituted the morning prayers, Isaac the afternoon prayers and Jacob the evening prayers.[1] In regard to the

---

1   "Thrice-daily prayer seems to have been an old Israelite tradition among the pious. Reference to it is found in Psalms (55:18) and in the book of Daniel (6:11). This practice is said to have been inspired by the three Patriarchs: Abraham, Isaac, and Jacob. According to *aggadic* interpretation of the verses (*Berakhot* 26b), the Torah tells of Abraham praying in the morning (Gen. 19:27), of Isaac praying towards dusk (Gen. 24:63), and of Jacob praying at night (Gen. 28:10)." [Donin, Hayim H., (1991). *To Pray as a Jew: A Guide*

morning prayers, it is written:

> And Abraham went early in the morning to the place where he had stood before the LORD. (Genesis 19:27)

> But I, O LORD, cry to you; in the morning my prayer comes before you."(Psalm 88:13)

> And rising very early in the morning, while it was still dark, he departed and went out to a desolate place, and there he prayed. (Mark 1:35)

In regard to the afternoon prayers it is written:

> And Isaac went out to meditate in the field toward evening. (Genesis 24:63)

> Now Peter and John were going up to the temple at the hour of prayer, the **ninth hour**. (Acts 3:1, emphasis added)

> At Caesarea there was a man named Cornelius, a centurion of what was known as the Italian Cohort, devout man who feared God with all his household, gave alms generously to the people, and prayed continually to God. About the **ninth hour**[2] of the day he saw clearly in a vision an angel of God... (Acts 10:1-3, emphasis added)

In regard to the evening prayers it is written:

> And he came to a certain place and stayed there that night, because the sun had set. (Genesis 28:11)

> Let my prayer be counted as incense before you, and the lifting up of my hands as the evening sacrifice! (Psalm 141:2)

---

to the Prayer Book and the Synagogue Service. Basic Books, 10.]

2 The ninth hour is representative of the afternoon (*mincha*) prayers. See Acts 10:30, where Cornelius says, "Four days ago, about this hour, I was praying in my house at the ninth hour..."

And after he had dismissed the crowds, he went up on the mountain by himself to pray. When evening came, he was there alone. (Matthew 14:23)

But our communication with God shouldn't end there. We should be continually speaking to him. The apostle Paul reminds us that we should be "praying at all times in the Spirit, with all prayer and supplication" (Ephesians 6:18). But how are we supposed to pray? Here are several examples of instruction on how we should pray:

> And when you pray, you must not be like the hypocrites. For they love to stand and pray in the synagogues and at the street corners, that they may be seen by others. Truly, I say to you, they have received their reward. But when you pray, go into your room and shut the door and pray to your Father who is in secret. And your Father who sees in secret will reward you. (Matthew 6:5-6)

> And when you pray, do not heap up empty phrases as the Gentiles do, for they think that they will be heard for their many words. (Matthew 6:7)

> Rabbi Shimon said … When you pray do not make your prayer a form of routine but a plea for mercy and supplications before G-d, for it is written (Joel 2:13), *For he is gracious and merciful, slow to anger, and abounding in steadfast love, and relents from punishing.* (Avot 2:18)

> Neither pray as the hypocrites, but as the Lord commanded in his gospel: *Our Father in heaven, hallowed be your name. Your kingdom come. Your will be done, as in heaven, so also on earth. Give us today our daily bread. And forgive us our debt, as we also forgive our debtors. And lead us not into temptation, but deliver us from evil, for yours is the power and the glory, forever.* Pray this way three times a day. (Didache 8:2-3)

> He [Judah ben Teima] used to pray: May it be thy will, O Lord our G-d and G-d of our fathers, that the Temple be rebuilt speedily in our days, and grant our portion in your Torah. (Avot 5:24)

Remember, the most important aspect of prayer is that it comes from our heart. This is called *kavannah*. Although there is no English equivalent for this Hebrew word, kavannah carries a meaning of heartfelt intentionality or focus. It is the difference between merely saying words and communicating with our Heavenly Father. When we pray, we need to make sure we are praying with kavannah.

Before the Maccabees went into battle or made an important decision, they always prayed and asked God for help. Before Yeshua did anything, he sought counsel from his Father. Shouldn't we do the same in our day-to-day lives? Shouldn't we seek the best advice in the universe for our daily decisions? Let's remember the lesson of the Three Candles, and offer up our prayers at the start of our day, the middle of our day and the end of our day.

Discussion

1. What do the Three Candles remind us of?

1. What is *tefillah*?

2. When are the set times of prayer and who gave them to us?

3. What does it mean to "pray like the hypocrites"?

4. What does it mean to "heap up empty phrases as the Gentiles do"?

5. How does Yeshua model prayer for us?

6. What areas in your life need more prayer?

7. What is the most important part of prayer?

Night Four

EMUNAH

Now therefore, O my sons, be zealous for the Torah, and give your lives for the covenant of your fathers and call to remembrance the works of the fathers, which they have done in their generations and you shall receive great glory, and an everlasting name. Was not Abraham found faithful in temptation, and it was reputed to him unto justice? Joseph in the time of his distress kept the commandment, and he was made lord of Egypt. Phineas our father, by being fervent in the zeal of God, received the covenant of an everlasting priesthood. Joshua, while he fulfilled the word, was made ruler in Israel. Caleb, for bearing witness before the congregation, received an inheritance. David by his mercy obtained the throne of an everlasting kingdom. Elijah, while he was full of zeal for the Torah, was taken up into heaven. Ananias and Azarias and Misael by believing, were delivered out of the flame. Daniel in his innocence was delivered out of the mouth of the lions. And thus consider through all generations that none that trust in him fail in strength. (1 Maccabees 2:50-61)

The fourth night of Hanukkah is here! We have four candles (and the shamash!) shining brightly from our hanukkiahs. Four flames are waiting to teach us an important lesson from the Maccabees and from our Master, Yeshua. Tonight, these Four Candles are here to remind us of the four Witnesses of our faith. They are here to teach us the importance of how the Four Gospels (Matthew, Mark, Luke and John) embolden our *emunah*, our faith. The Gospels are the four testimonies of Yeshua in regard to his life, his teachings, his ministry, his power, his authority, his death, burial and resurrection, as well as his promised return. *Gospel* means "good news." We have four accounts of the good news of Yeshua.

You see, in order to believe in someone or something, we first need to know about that someone or something. Through the Gospel record we come to know about Yeshua and his life-changing message and ministry. The prophet Joel says, "everyone who calls on the name of the Lord shall be saved" (Joel 2:32). Paul, reflecting on this promise, asks this question:

> How then will they call on him in whom they have not believed? And how are they to believe in him of whom they have never heard? And how are they to hear without someone preaching? And how are they to preach unless they are sent? As it is written, "How beautiful are the feet of those who preach the good news!" (Romans 10:14-15)

He answers by saying that faith—emunah—comes to a person through hearing the testimony of our Messiah: "So faith comes from hearing, and hearing through the word of Christ" (Romans 10:17).

We have been provided with four testimonies—each one with details distinct from the others—that serve as faithful witnesses of the life of our Messiah. Building upon and complementing the others, each perspective helps establish our emunah in regard to our Messiah. The author of the book of Hebrews also speaks of emunah:

> Now faith is the assurance of things hoped for, the conviction of things not seen. For by it the people of old received their commendation. By faith we understand that the universe was created by the word of God, so that what is seen was not made out of things that are visible. (Hebrews 11:1-3)

He continues with a long list of examples of emunah being displayed by men and women in the Holy Scriptures. He begins his list:

"By faith Abel ..."
"By faith Enoch ..."
"By faith Noah ..."
"By faith Abraham ..."
"By faith Sarah ..."
"By faith Isaac ..."
"By faith Jacob ..."
"By faith Joseph ..."
"By faith Moses ..."
"By faith Rahab ..."

He concludes by saying his list could go on and on:

> And what more shall I say? For time would fail me to tell of Gideon, Barak, Samson, Jephthah, of David and Samuel and the prophets— who through faith conquered kingdoms, enforced justice, obtained promises, stopped the mouths of lions, quenched the power of fire, escaped the edge of the sword, were made strong out of weakness, became mighty in war, put foreign armies to flight. (Hebrews 11:32-34)

The Maccabees were part of a long succession of Israelites who continued in this legacy of faith. Just as their fathers before them, they too "quenched the power of fire, escaped the edge of the sword, were made strong out of weakness, became mighty in war, put foreign armies to flight." They fought the fight of faith, refusing to allow doubt or hypocrisy to sway them from their path. But we must remember that emunah is more than just acknowledging or agreeing with something. It is a conviction that motivates action. It is belief that results in faithfulness. As a matter of fact, the author of Hebrews says that without faith it is literally impossible to please God (Hebrews 11:6).

Scripture places great emphasis on faith and how it drives our entire life; it is the focal point of several important teachings. Paul connects the good news of Yeshua with faith and a rejuvenated life of righteousness when he says the following:

> For I am not ashamed of the gospel, for it is the power of God for salvation to everyone who believes, to the Jew first and also to the Greek. For in it the righteousness of God is revealed from faith for faith, as it is written, "The righteous shall live by faith." (Romans 1:16-17)

The end of the matter is that we need to be a part of this unbroken chain of faith as well. We need to allow our faith in Yeshua to drive us to live every moment of our lives on his behalf.

> Therefore, since we are surrounded by so great a cloud of witnesses, let us also lay aside every weight, and sin which clings so closely, and let us run with endurance the race that is set before us, looking to Jesus, the founder and perfecter of our faith, who for the joy that was set before him endured

the cross, despising the shame, and is seated at the right hand of the throne of God. (Hebrews 12:1–2)

So, let's remember the lesson of the Four Lights: There are Four Gospels that witness to the Good News of our Master, and that Good News should result in a life of emunah within us.

Discussion

1. What do the Four Lights remind us of?

2. How does emunah come to a person?

3. How does the author of the book of Hebrews define emunah?

4. Who are some of the examples of emunah listed in the book of Hebrews?

5. How does our belief affect our actions?

6. How do the Maccabees represent emunah?

7. What are some practical ways we can show our emunah?

Night Five
TESHUVAH

And they fasted that day, and put on haircloth, and put ashes upon their heads and they rent their garments ... And they cried with a loud voice toward heaven ... (1 Maccabees 3:47, 50)

One, two, three, four, five bright candles glowing from our hanukkiah. Tonight, the fifth night of the Festival of Lights, the candles will teach us a lesson that was at the heart of Yeshua's ministry:

"Repent! For the Kingdom of Heaven is at hand!" (Matthew 4:17)

These were the words of our Master as he walked to and fro along the countryside of the Galilee and the hills of Judea. This was his good news, his gospel message that he preached among the people of Israel. His life and ministry were centered around *teshuvah*, repentance. He constantly worked toward helping people understand this crucial message.

Close your eyes with me for a moment. Use your imagination. Can you see him walking along the road, calling out to all who would hear? Can you hear his voice, thick with his Galilean accent, crying out, "*Shuvu! Ki Malchut HaShammayim karvah lavo!*" Can you see the faces of those he passes? Some are frightened. Some are mocking. Some are weeping. But none of them can ignore this man from Nazareth speaking directly to their souls.

But what does it mean to repent? Repentance means more than asking for forgiveness. And although repentance begins with remorse, it does not end there. Repentance is a call to action. Through repentance we can attain a higher spiritual position than someone who does not need to repent. The sages tell us:

> Completely righteous people cannot stand in the place where someone who has repented stands. (Berachot 34b)

Yeshua alludes to this concept when he says, "Just so, I tell you, there will be more joy in heaven over one sinner who repents than over ninety-nine righteous persons who need no repentance" (Luke 5:7).

Teshuvah means more than just admitting your wrongdoing. It means turning completely around and going in a direction opposite of the path you were previously on. It means righting the wrongs you have caused in another person's life. It means submitting your life to the kingship of the King of Kings. In a nutshell it means to return. But return to what?

One, two, three, four, five. Five are the books of Torah. This is the foundation from which all subsequent revelation flows. The Torah, the foundation of our faith, is the standard by which all other truth is measured. And it is this Torah to which teshuvah—repentance—is anchored. When Yeshua tells us to repent, he is telling us to return to the righteous standard of the Torah and its wisdom, rather than continue living by our own standard. When Yeshua says, "Repent! For the Kingdom of Heaven is at hand!" he is saying, "Turn around from the path you are on! Come back to the righteous ways of the Torah! Accept my kingship upon you and be my disciple!"

This is the secret to true spirituality. Only through constant repentance can we have spiritual eyes that see beyond the physical reality. Only through repentance can we see the need for healing in our world. The sages taught that repentance can actually bring that healing to the world:

> Great is repentance, for it brings healing to the world, as it is said: I will heal their affliction, generously will I take them back in love [Hosea 14:5]." [3]

How powerful is repentance?

Rabbi Simon states: "When a man shoots an arrow, how far will it travel? Over one or two fields. The power of repentance is so great, however, that it reaches the throne of glory!" In a similar vein, Rabbi Yose comments: "God has declared, 'Make for me an opening as an eye of a needle, and I will open

---

[3] As quoted by Rabbi Hama, the son of Hanina in b. *Yoma* 86a

it for you so wide, that armies of soldiers with heavy equipment can enter through it.'" (Pesik. Rab Kah. 5:6; 24:12).[4]

How important is repentance? In the book of Revelation, Yeshua tells us:

> Remember, then, what you received and heard. Keep it, and repent. If you will not wake up, I will come like a thief, and you will not know at what hour I will come against you. (Revelation 3:3)

The Scriptures are filled with the message of repentance. The prophets longed for the day when Israel would turn back to the Lord and to His Torah whole-heartedly. This is the central message of the Bible, the over-arching voice that cries to be heard. It calls out, "Turn around, my Beloved! Return to your first love!"

This is the message to the Jewish people. But what about non-Jews? Why is repentance particularly important to non-Jews? Repentance changes our citizenship from one kingdom to another. Through repentance and submission to Yeshua, we are transferred from the Kingdom of Darkness into the Kingdom of Light. This amazed the apostles; they didn't realize Yeshua's message would extend beyond the Jewish people. The book of Acts records their reaction:

> When they heard these things they fell silent. And they glorified God, saying, "Then to the Gentiles also God has granted repentance that leads to life." (Acts 11:18)

One, two, three, four, five. Five little candles. Five little books. One little turn that will forever change our destiny. Torah. Yeshua. Teshuvah ... Life.

---

[4] Brad H. Young, *Meet the Rabbis: Rabbinic Thought and the Teachings of Jesus* (Hendrickson Publishers, 2007-06-30), 23.

Discussion

1. What do the five candles remind us of?

2. What is teshuvah?

3. What was the "good news" that Yeshua preached?

4. What is repentance?

5. How does the Torah call us to repentance?

6. What did Rabbi Yose mean when he made his statement about the eye of a needle?

7. What were the apostles amazed about in Acts 11?

Night Six
ANAVAH

And behold the nations are come together against us to destroy us. You know what they intend against us. How shall we be able to stand before their face, unless you, O God, help us? ... For it is better for us to die in battle, than to see the evils of our nation, and of the holies. Nevertheless as it shall be the will of God in heaven so be it done. (1 Maccabees 3:52-53, 59-60)

Six candles. Six lights. Six—the number of humanity shines brightly this night. Yes, the number six reminds us of imperfection, of humanity. After all, man was created on the sixth day, just before God ceased from his labors. Man was made from the dust of the earth. He is a living being formed from the "stuff" of earth: an EARTH-ling. He is tied to this world through his flesh. His main "ingredient" is the element carbon. Carbon is made up of six protons, six neutrons and six electrons. It is a constant reminder that this existence is only temporal.

This reminder gives us the proper perspective on life. We are reminded that this life will one day come to an end and we must make the most of the time we have been allotted. *Anavah*—humility—is the secret to making each moment count. Let me explain.

When you hear the word *humility*, what comes to mind? Too many times our working definition of humility is self-abasement. My new "2.0" definition of humility comes from a book by Alen Morinis called *Everyday Holiness*. My paraphrase of his definition is as follows:

Humility is occupying our proper space, neither too much, nor too little.[5]

---

5   Alan Morinis, *Everyday Holiness: The Jewish Spiritual Path of Mussar* (Trumpeter, 2008-12-02), 45.

I think this is the best definition of humility I've ever heard. It makes sense on so many levels. When we break down a character trait into such a definition, we are able to truly define its parameters. Let's explore this definition for a moment.

If humility is "occupying our proper space, neither too much, nor too little," and we occupy too much space, the result is obvious: We become so wrapped up in ourselves that the boundaries between us and others are unseen. We quickly overstep those boundaries and invade someone else's space, whether physically, socially or verbally.

John the Immerser wanted to make sure he didn't overstep the boundary of prominence between himself and Yeshua. When someone came to him indignant that Yeshua and his disciples were immersing even more people than John and his disciples were, John's response was, "He must increase, but I must decrease" (John 3:30). This should be our attitude as well. We should be quick to give others credit even when we feel we deserve it. Yeshua tells us:

> "When you are invited by someone to a wedding feast, do not sit down in a place of honor, lest someone more distinguished than you be invited by him, and he who invited you both will come and say to you, 'Give your place to this person,' and then you will begin with shame to take the lowest place. But when you are invited, go and sit in the lowest place, so that when your host comes he may say to you, 'Friend, move up higher.' Then you will be honored in the presence of all who sit at table with you. For everyone who exalts himself will be humbled, and he who humbles himself will be exalted." (Luke 14:8-11)

He desires for us to consider others before ourselves and allow our actions to demonstrate that consideration. In Romans 12, before beginning a long list of things of how believers should live, Paul makes this appeal:

> "I say to everyone among you not to think of himself more highly than he ought to think, but to think with sober judgment, each according to the measure of faith that God has assigned." (Romans 12:3)

Paul takes this lesson from Moses, whom Scripture notes as "very humble, more than all people who were on the face of the earth" (Numbers 12:3). According to the sages, Moses even demonstrated his humility in how he wrote out the letters of the Torah. For example, the book of Leviticus is called *Vayikra* in Hebrew. Vayikra means "and he called," which refers to God calling out to Moses from the Tent of Meeting. In a *Sefer Torah*—a Torah scroll—there is a letter written smaller than the rest. This letter is the *aleph*, the first letter in the Hebrew word *ani*, which means "I." The sages say that as Moses wrote this word, he reduced the size of the letter *aleph* because he still could not believe that the Creator of the universe spoke to him "face to face, as a man speaks to his friend" (Exodus 33:11).

But what about when we don't occupy enough space, the space we are supposed to occupy? If this happens, then someone else has to step in and take up the slack. We all have our special role to play. If we don't fill up our allotted space, we are destined to fail others who rely on us—we are not fulfilling our God-given role in the world.

Hillel said, "In a place where there are no men strive to be a man" (Avot 2:6). We must step up to the plate and fill the role intended for us. God has a calling for each one of us. We must not run from it, nor must we overstep our boundaries and land in the space of another person. As we read in the introducton to today's devotion, the Maccabees balanced their understanding of God's sovereignty with their responsibility. They said, "How shall we be able to stand before their face, unless thou, O God, help us? ... For it is better for us to die in battle, than to see the evils of our nation, and of the holies." They knew they must fight, but they knew that it was really the Almighty who would win the victory.

So, let these six candles remind us that, although we are destined to wither away like the flowers and the grass, we have a responsibility in this life that only we can fulfill. Anavah—humility—will keep us on that path of fulfillment.

Discussion
1. What does the number six represent?
2. What does *anavah* mean?
3. What new definition of humility did we learn?
4. How did Moses exemplify humility?
5. How did Yeshua exemplify humility?
6. How does not occupying our proper space affect others?
7. What are some practical ways we can be more humble?

Night Seven
TZEDAKAH

> But there were no provisions in the city, because it was the seventh year and such as had stayed in Judea of them that came from among the nations, had eaten the residue of all that which had been stored up. And there remained in the holy places but a few, for the famine had prevailed over them and they were dispersed every man to his own place. (1 Maccabees 6:53–54)

Seven glowing candles plus our shamash tell us that tonight is the seventh night of Hanukkah! Each night, the brightness and warmth of our hanukkiah have grown with the addition of a new candle.

Numerous biblical themes are associated with the number seven. There were seven days of Creation, therefore there are seven days of the week. There are seven days of Unleavened Bread and seven days of *Sukkot* (Tabernacles). The High Holy Days fall in the seventh month of the biblical calendar. *Shavuot* (Pentecost) comes seven weeks after *Pesach* (Passover). The *Shmitta* (the Sabbatical year) falls every seven years. There are seven lights on a normal menorah. The list goes on and on. Let's turn our attention, however, to an event found in the Apostolic Scriptures.

The Gospel of Matthew records for us a time when Yeshua was teaching in a remote area of the Galilee. The crowds, hanging on his every word, had been with him for three days and refused to leave. Just before sending the crowds back to their homes, Yeshua tells his disciples to feed them because he doesn't want them to leave and possibly collapse along their way. He asked his disciples, "How many loaves do you have?" They responded, "Seven, and a few small fish." Here's what follows:

> And directing the crowd to sit down on the ground, he took the seven loaves and the fish, and having given thanks he broke them and gave them to the

disciples, and the disciples gave them to the crowds. And they all ate and were satisfied. And they took up seven baskets full of the broken pieces left over. Those who ate were four thousand men, besides women and children. (Matthew 15:34–38)

Our Master was moved with compassion for the welfare of those around him. He considered it his obligation to provide sustenance for them before he sent them away. Not only that, but he wanted to teach his disciples the principle of giving to those in need. Sure, they had grown up learning and practicing this principle, but not to the extent Yeshua taught them. He emphasized the need to help alleviate human suffering, and explained that our generosity and compassion toward others is a thermometer of our spiritual health. He taught us:

> The eye is the lamp of the body. So, if your eye is healthy, your whole body will be full of light, but if your eye is bad, your whole body will be full of darkness. If then the light in you is darkness, how great is the darkness! (Matthew 6:22–23)

Most people misunderstand this passage and don't realize he was speaking about generosity, because he used a Hebrew idiom we don't catch in either the English or the Greek. In Hebrew, the eye is the organ of the body associated with generosity, rather than our English concept of a "generous heart" (see Proverbs 22:9; 23:6; Matthew 20:15). He specifically taught that his disciples should be some of the most giving people on earth.

At the beginning of this chapter Yeshua taught how his disciples should give:

> Beware of practicing your righteousness before other people in order to be seen by them, for then you will have no reward from your Father who is in heaven ... But when you give to the needy, do not let your left hand know what your right hand is doing, so that your giving may be in secret. And your Father who sees in secret will reward you. (Matthew 6:1, 3–4)

In this passage, Yeshua didn't use the term "righteousness" (*tzedakah*) in the normal, biblical sense of justice. Instead, he used it synonymously with "charity," just as the rabbis do. Why is this? It's similar to the metamorphosis of our

English word *charity*. Originally, the word *charity* meant "love." In fact, this is how the King James Bible uses it. Over time, though, "charity" became synonymous with taking care of the needy, because to truly love someone is to love them in deed, rather than merely in word. The word *tzedakah*—"righteousness"—underwent a similar transformation because of how it was associated with taking care of the poor. The LORD declared through the prophet Jeremiah that to take care of the poor and needy is to do "justice and righteousness," and is, in fact, the essence of what it means to know Him:

> Do justice and righteousness, and deliver from the hand of the oppressor him who has been robbed ... Did not your father eat and drink and do justice and righteousness? Then it was well with him. He judged the cause of the poor and needy; then it was well. Is not this to know me? declares the Lord. (Jeremiah 22:3, 15–16)

Within Judaism, giving to those in need is not looked upon as an act of generosity, but merely an act of justice and righteousness. As we have seen, this is the very definition of the word tzedakah. In fact, tzedakah does not even belong to us; it belongs to the LORD. The midrash explains that when we withhold tzedakah from the needy, we are actually robbing him of what God has already given to him:

> Sufficient for him is his poverty. Is it not enough for the rich man that he is in easy circumstances while the poor man is in distress, but that he must needs rob him also of what the Holy One, blessed be He, has given him? (Numbers Rabbah 5:2).

This sounds a lot like the words of our Master in Matthew 25:31-46 where he teaches that what we do to "the least of these" is, in reality, done to him. Therefore, if we feed, clothe and take care of the needy or visit them when they are sick or incarcerated, it is as if we did so for Yeshua. On the Last Day, the Judge will say to us, "Come, you who are blessed by my Father, inherit the kingdom prepared for you from the foundation of the world" (verse 34). Yeshua tells us the opposite is true also. If we neglect to do these things, we neglect Yeshua as well. The Judge's response will be, "Truly, I say to you, as you did not do it to one of the least of these, you did not do it to me" (verse 45). Yeshua's conclusion is, "These will go away into eternal punishment, but the righteous into eternal life." (verse 46).

Judaism teaches that tzedakah is limited to a certain percentage of our income. Yeshua, however, instructs us to give without limitation knowing our Heavenly Father sees and will repay us—as Proverbs 19:17 says, "Whoever is generous to the poor lends to the Lord, and he will repay him for his deed." He says, "Give to the one who begs from you, and do not refuse the one who would borrow from you" (Matthew 5:42). Yeshua's teaching may be based on his interpretation of Proverbs 3:27-28, which says the following:

> Do not withhold good from those to whom it is due, when it is in your power to do it. Do not say to your neighbor, "Go, and come again, tomorrow I will give it"—when you have it with you.

Whatever the case, he wants us to give beyond our normal comforts and rely upon our Heavenly Father for our own needs. In the conclusion of his discourse about our dependence on God, Yeshua says, "But seek first the kingdom of God and his righteousness, and all these things will be added to you" (Matthew 6:33). What does he mean? He means that when we give tzedakah and take care of others, our Heavenly Father's tzedakah will be sufficient to sustain us, because it cannot be exhausted.

As I stated in the introduction, it is traditional to give tzedakah on a festival. It reminds us there are always those less fortunate than ourselves and gives us an opportunity to partner with the Holy One to bring repair to this world (see tomorrow night's devotional for more details on this). Tzedakah is partnering with the Holy One to help complete what is lacking in others. Let's not forget to put into practice what we have learned on this seventh night of Hanukkah.

As we pray on Rosh Hashanah, "*Teshuvah* (repentance), *tefillah* (prayer) and *tzedakah* (righteousness/charity) annul the evil decree." May our tzedakah be lifted before the Holy One as we imitate our Master by helping meet the needs of those around us.

Discussion

1. What events in the Scriptures correspond to the number seven?

2. What is tzedakah?

3. What does tzedakah literally mean?

4. How did the meaning of this word change over time?

5. What event in the life of Yeshua did we discuss as a model for tzedakah?

6. How do we honor God by giving tzedakah?

7. What are some creative ways to give tzedakah?

Night Eight

TIKKUN OLAM

And Simon ... cast them out of the city, and cleansed the houses wherein there had been idols, and then he entered into it with hymns, blessing the Lord. And having cast out of it all uncleanness, he placed in it men that should observe the Torah and he fortified it, and made it his habitation. (1 Maccabees 13:47–48)

Tonight, the last night of Hanukkah, eight small candles (and the shamash!) are ablaze on our hanukkiah, casting their light on smiling faces and cheerful hearts. Although it may seem that the festivities come to an end tonight, it is really a beginning of sorts. You see, the number eight is the number associated with new beginnings. Last night we briefly listed out several things in the Bible that corresponded to the number seven. One of these is the very first group of seven in the entire Bible ... the days of Creation. This, of course, is where we get our days of the week. We number the days of the week according to the days of Creation. There were seven days of Creation, therefore we have seven days in our week.

But what happens after those seven days are up? What happens after Sabbath? Do our days end? Are there no more days or weeks left to experience? By no means! Once we have experienced all seven of those days, we start the cycle all over again. We mark the division of sacred and secular time with a ceremony called *Havdalah* ("separation") and then we start with Day One all over again. But have you ever thought about the beginning of the following week to be not Day One, but Day Eight? Yes, it is a new week, but it is in many ways a continuation of the previous week. Time does not stop. It is perpetual, without end. Let me give you an example of what I mean.

In the Torah, the LORD requires all Jewish males to be circumcised as a reminder of His covenant with them. However, the circumcision is to take place specifically eight days after their birth. Eight full days are to elapse between birth and the circumcision. Why is this? Possibly, so that the child will have lived out each one of the seven days of the week prior to his circumcision. Only when he has experienced all seven days of the weekly cycle is he subjected to the covenantal sign of circumcision. He has completed an entire week and begun another. In a sense, through this process, the cycle of life has been renewed. Here's another example.

Every year the Torah is read from Genesis through Deuteronomy. This process takes an entire year to complete. But does it merely end when it's completed? No. Once we have completed reading Deuteronomy, we immediately roll back the scroll and begin reading Genesis again. What day is this done on? Outside of Israel, it's on a day called *Simchat Torah* ("the Joy of the Torah"). But in Israel, it is done on a day called *Shemini Atzeret*. What does this mean? It means the "Eighth Day Assembly." The Torah reading is concluded and begun anew on the eighth day counting from the beginning of *Sukkot* (the Feast of Tabernacles). The seven days have been completed, and it is time for something new to begin.

Something similar happened in the life of our Master. When he willingly gave up his physical life, his life didn't end there. He took it up again. When did he raise from the grave? We typically say his resurrection took place on the first day of the week. But in light of our discussion, we can also say he was raised on the Eighth Day. It was a new beginning not only for him, but for all of his followers as well. His resurrection marked the beginning of something new and incredible. His resurrection set things in motion for our resurrection. Paul tells us one day "this perishable body must put on the imperishable, and this mortal body must put on immortality" (1 Corinthians 15:53). That which has been corrupted (the flesh) will one day be made incorruptible because of the victory of our Master over death.

But what about now? Yeshua tells us that, through accepting the yoke of his kingship, we can experience a portion of the resurrection now. We can enter into that eternal Kingdom and experience "life abundant" now. His gospel message was, "Repent! For the Kingdom of Heaven is at hand!" He desires us to turn from our own ways, accept his kingship and partner with him to bring repair to this world—now, in this life. As we learned on the fifth night, Yeshua preached teshuvah (repentance), the first step in repairing the damaged relationship between us and our Creator. But we must go beyond this and bring a restoration to others as well. We must work in conjunction with the Almighty towards repairing a fallen world, as Paul teaches us in 2 Corinthians:

> All this is from God, who through Christ reconciled us to himself and gave us the ministry of reconciliation; that is, in Christ God was reconciling the world to himself, not counting their trespasses against them, and entrusting to us the message of reconciliation. (2 Corinthians 5:18-19)

In Hebrew, the concept of bringing repair to the world is called *tikkun olam* ("repair of the world"). Just as our Master repaired the damage in this world caused by sin, our job is to partner with him to continue this mission until his return. In fact, he taught us to pray, "Your Kingdom come, Your will be done on earth as it is in Heaven" (Matthew 6:10). This is the foundation for our mission of tikkun olam. Everything we do, everything we say, should partner with the Father to bring this world in alignment with His Eternal Kingdom.

How do we do this? We remember the Eight Lights of Hanukkah:

1. **SERVE (*Avodah*)** others selflessly
2. **LOVE (*Ahavah*)** others deeply
3. **PRAY (*Tefillah*)** consistently and fervently
4. Live lives of **FAITH** and **FAITHFULNESS (*Emunah*)**
5. Quickly and continually **REPENT (*Teshuvah*)** when we fall into sin
6. Walk **HUMBLY (*Anavah*)** before the Lord
7. Give **CHARITY (*Tzedakah*)** to those in need

When we do these things, we partner with the Holy One to shine our light through the darkness (Matthew 5:16) and bring *tikkun* (repair) to this fallen world. Once the repairs are complete, then we will be able to celebrate and rejoice in the works of the LORD as the Macabbees did:

> And they kept the dedication of the altar eight days, and they offered burnt offerings with joy, and sacrifices of salvation, and of praise... And Judah, and his brethren, and all the church of Israel decreed, that the day of the dedication of the altar should be kept in its season from year to year for eight days, from the five and twentieth day of the month of Kislev, with joy and gladness. (1 Maccabees 4:56, 59)

Only after Judah and his brothers restored the Holy Temple, repaired and rededicated the altar to the service of the Holy One did the celebrations begin. Let us work towards tikkun olam so that we may be able to rejoice with our Creator once more.

Discussion

1. How are the numbers 1 and 8 related?

2. What is the number 8 a symbol of?

3. What special events happened in the life of Yeshua on the "eighth" day?

4. What is tikkun olam and how does it take place?

5. How does Yeshua's prayer set our direction in regard to tikkun olam?

6. What are some ways we can partner with Yeshua to bring tikkun olam to this world?

7. How should Yeshua's resurrection motivate us towards tikkun olam?

CHAPTER FOUR
Remember

1 Maccabees: The Story of Hanukkah

MODIFIED FROM THE DOUAY-RHEIMS 1899 AMERICAN EDITION

CHAPTER 1

From Alexander to Antiochus.

Now it came to pass, after that Alexander the son of Philip the Macedonian, who first reigned in Greece, coming out of the land of Kittim, had overthrown Darius king of the Persians and Medes. He fought many battles, and took the strongholds of all, and slew the kings of the earth. And he went through even to the ends of the earth, and took the spoils of many nations, and the earth was quiet before him. He gathered a power and a very strong army, and his heart was exalted and lifted up. He subdued countries of nations and princes, and they became tributaries to him. After these things, he fell down upon his bed and knew that he should die. And he called his servants the nobles that were brought up with him from his youth, and he divided his kingdom among them while he was yet alive. Alexander reigned twelve years and he died. And his servants made themselves kings every one in his place. They all put crowns upon themselves after his death, and their sons after them many years, and evils were multiplied in the earth. And there came out of them a wicked root, Antiochus the Illustrious, the son of King Antiochus, who had been a hostage at Rome, and he reigned in the hundred and thirty-seventh year of the kingdom of the Greeks.

Lawless Jews.

In those days there went out of Israel wicked men, and they persuaded many, saying, "Let us go, and make a covenant with the heathens that are round about us; for since we departed from them, many evils have befallen us." And the word seemed good in their eyes. And some of the people determined to do this and went to the king, and he gave them license to do after the ordinances of the heathens. They built a place of exercise in Jerusalem, according to the laws of the nations. And they made themselves foreskins, and departed from the holy covenant and joined themselves to the heathens and were sold to do evil.

Antiochus in Egypt.

And the kingdom was established before Antiochus, and he had a mind to reign over the land of Egypt, that he might reign over two kingdoms. He entered into Egypt with a great multitude, with chariots and elephants, and horsemen, and a great number of ships. And he made war against Ptolemy king of Egypt, but Ptolemy was afraid at his presence and fled, and many were wounded unto death. And he took the strong cities in the land of Egypt, and took the spoils of the land.

Robbery of the Temple.

After Antiochus had ravaged Egypt in the hundred and forty-third year, he returned and went up against Israel. And he went up to Jerusalem with a great multitude. And he proudly entered into the sanctuary, and took away the golden altar, and the candlestick of light, and all the vessels thereof, and the table of proposition, and the pouring vessels, and the vials, and the little mortars of gold, and the veil, and the crowns, and the golden ornament that was before the Temple, and he broke them all in pieces. He took the silver and gold and the precious vessels, and he took the hidden treasures which he found, and when he had taken all away he departed into his own country. And he made a great slaughter of men, and spoke very proudly. And there was great mourning in Israel, and in every place where they were. The princes and the ancients mourned, and the virgins and the young men were made feeble, and the beauty of the women was changed. Every bridegroom took up lamentation and the bride that sat in the marriage bed, mourned. And the land was moved for the inhabitants thereof, and all the house of Jacob was covered with confusion.

Attack and Occupation.

And after two full years the king sent the chief collector of his tributes to the cities of Judea, and he came to Jerusalem with a great multitude. And he spoke to them peaceable words in deceit, and they believed him. And he fell upon the city suddenly, and struck it with a great slaughter, and destroyed much people in Israel. And he took the spoils of the city, and burnt it with fire, and threw down the houses thereof, and the walls thereof round about. They took the women captive, and the children, and the cattle they possessed. And they built the city of David with a great and strong wall, and with strong towers, and made it a fortress for them. And they placed there a sinful nation, wicked men, and they fortified themselves therein and stored up armor and provisions, and gathered together the spoils of Jerusalem, and laid them up there, and they became a great snare. This was a place to lie in wait against the sanctuary, and an evil devil in Israel. And they shed innocent blood round about the sanctuary, and defiled the holy place. The inhabitants of Jerusalem fled away by reason of them, and the city was made the habitation of strangers, and she became a stranger to her own seed, and her children forsook her. Her sanctuary was desolate like a wilderness, her festival days were turned into mourning, her Sabbaths into reproach, her honors were brought to nothing. Her dishonor was increased according to her glory, and her excellency was turned into mourning.

Religious Persecution.

And King Antiochus wrote to all his kingdom, that all the people should be one and every one should leave his own law. And all nations consented according to the word of King Antiochus. And many of Israel consented to his service, and they sacrificed to idols, and profaned the Sabbath. The king sent letters by the hands of messengers to Jerusalem, and to all the cities of Judea, that they should follow the law of the nations of the earth, and should forbid burnt offerings and sacrifices and atonements to be made in the Temple of God, and should prohibit the Sabbath and the festival days to be celebrated. And he commanded the holy places to be profaned, and the holy people of Israel. He commanded altars and temples and idols to be built, and swine's flesh and unclean beasts to be sacrificed. And that they should leave their children uncircumcised, and let their souls be defiled with all uncleannesses and abominations, to the end that they should forget the Torah and should change all the ordinances of God. And that whosoever would not do according to the word of King Antiochus should be put to death.

According to all these words he wrote to his whole kingdom, and he appointed rulers over the people that should force them to do these things. And they commanded the cities of Judea to sacrifice. Then many of the people were gathered to them that had forsaken the Torah of the Lord and they committed evils in the land. And they drove away the people of Israel into lurking holes, and into the secret places of fugitives. On the fifteenth day of the month Kislev, in the hundred and forty-fifth year, King Antiochus set up the abominable idol of desolation upon the altar of God, and they built altars throughout all the cities of Judea round about, and they burnt incense and sacrificed at the doors of the houses and in the streets. They cut in pieces and burnt with fire the books of the Torah of God. And every one with whom the books of the testament of the Lord were found, and whosoever observed the Torah of the Lord, they put to death, according to the edict of the king. Thus by their power did they deal with the people of Israel that were found in the cities month after month. And on the twenty-fifth day of the month they sacrificed upon the altar of the idol that was over against the altar of God. Now the women that circumcised their children, were slain according to the commandment of King Antiochus. And they hanged the children about their necks in all their houses, andthose that had circumcised them were put to death. Many of the people of Israel determined with themselves that they would not eat unclean things, and they chose rather to die than to be defiled with unclean meats. They would not break the holy covenant of God, and they were put to death. And there was very great wrath upon the people.

Chapter 2

Mattathias and His Sons.

In those days arose Mathathias, the son of John, the son of Simeon, a priest of the sons of Joarib, from Jerusalem, and he abode in the mountain of Modin. And he had five sons: John who was surnamed Gaddis; Simon, who was surnamed Thasi; Judah, who was called Machabeus; Eleazar, who was surnamed Abaron; and Jonathan, who was surnamed Apphus. These saw the evils that were done in the people of Judea, and in Jerusalem. And Mathathias said:

> Woe is me, wherefore was I born to see the ruin of my people, and the ruin of the holy city, and to dwell there, when it is given into the hands of the enemies? The holy places are come into the hands of strangers; her Temple is become as a man without honor. The vessels of her glory are carried away captive, her old men are murdered in the streets, and her young men are fallen by the sword of the enemies. What nation has not inherited her kingdom, and gotten of her spoils? All her ornaments are taken away. She that was free is made a slave. And behold our sanctuary, and our beauty, and our glory is laid waste, and the Gentiles have defiled them. To what end then should we live any longer?

And Mathathias and his sons rent their garments, and they covered themselves with haircloth, and made great lamentation.

Pagan Worship Refused and Resisted.
And they that were sent from King Antiochus came thither, to compel them that were fled into the city of Modin, to sacrifice, and to burn incense, and to depart from the Torah of God. And many of the people of Israel consented, and came to them, but Mathathias and his sons stood firm. And they that were sent from Antiochus, answering, said to Mathathias: "You are a ruler, and an honorable and great man in this city, and adorned with sons and brethren. Therefore, come first and obey the king's commandment, as all nations and the men of Judea have done, and they that remain in Jerusalem, and you and your sons, shall be in the number of the king's friends and enriched with gold, silver, and many presents. Then Mathathias answered, and said with a loud voice:

> Although all nations obey King Antiochus, so as to depart every man from the service of the law of his fathers, and consent to his commandments: I and my sons, and my brethren will obey the Torah of our fathers. God be merciful unto us; it is not profitable for us to forsake the Torah and the laws of God. We will not hearken to the words of King Antiochus, neither will we sacrifice and transgress the commandments of our Torah to go another way.

Now as he left off speaking these words, there came a certain Jew in the sight of all to sacrifice to the idols upon the altar in the city of Modin, according to the king's commandment. And Mathathias saw and was grieved, and his reins trembled, and his wrath was kindled according to the judgment of the Torah, and running upon him he slew him upon the altar. Moreover the man whom King Antiochus had sent, who compelled them to sacrifice, he slew at the same time, and pulled down the altar and shewed zeal for the Torah, as Phineas did by Zimri the son of Salomi. And Mathathias cried out in the city with a loud voice, saying, "Every one that has zeal for the Torah, and maintains the testament, let him follow me!" So he and his sons fled to the mountains and left all that they had in the city. Then many that sought after judgment, and justice, went down into the desert and they abode there, they and their children and their wives and their cattle, because afflictions increased upon them.

And it was told to the king's men, and to the army that was in Jerusalem in the city of David, that certain men who had broken the king's commandment, were gone away into the secret places in the wilderness, and that many were gone after them. Forthwith they went out towards them, and made war against them on the Sabbath day. And they said to them, "Do you still resist? Come forth, and do according to the edict of King Antiochus, and you shall live." And they said, "We will not come forth, neither will we obey the king's edict, to profane the Sabbath day." And they made haste to give them battle. But they answered them not, neither did they cast a stone at them, nor stopped up the secret places, saying, "Let us all die in our innocence and heaven and earth shall be witnesses for us, that you put us to death wrongfully." So they gave them battle on the Sabbath and they were slain with their wives and their children and their cattle, to the number of a thousand persons.

And Mathathias and his friends heard of it, and they mourned for them exceedingly. And every man said to his neighbor, "If we shall all do as our brethren have done, and not fight against the heathens for our lives, and our ordinances, they will now quickly root us out of the earth." And they determined in that day, saying, "Whosoever shall come up against us to fight on the Sabbath day, we will fight against him and we will not all die, as our brethren that were slain in the secret places." Then was assembled to them the congregation of the Assideans, the stoutest of Israel, every one that had a good will for the Torah. All who fled from the evils joined themselves to them and were a support to them. They gathered an army and slew the sinners in their wrath and the wicked men in their indignation, and the rest fled to the nations for safety. And Mathathias and his friends went round about, and they threw down the altars and circumcised all the children whom they found in the confines of Israel that were uncircumcised, and they did valiantly. And they pursued after the children of pride, and the work prospered in their hands; they recovered the Torah out of the hands of the nations and out of the hands of the kings, and they yielded not the horn to the sinner.

Farewell of Mattathias.

Now the days drew near that Mathathias should die, and he said to his sons:

> Now has pride and chastisement gotten strength, and the time of destruction, and the wrath of indignation. Now therefore, O my sons, be zealous for the Torah, and give your lives for the covenant of your fathers and call to remembrance the works of the fathers, which they have done in their generations, and you shall receive great glory, and an everlasting name. Was not Abraham found faithful in temptation, and it was reputed to him unto righteousness? Joseph in the time of his distress kept the commandment, and he was made lord of Egypt. Phineas our father, by being fervent in the zeal of God, received the covenant of an everlasting priesthood. Joshua, while he fulfilled the word, was made ruler in Israel. Caleb,

for bearing witness before the congregation, received an inheritance. David by his mercy obtained the throne of an everlasting kingdom. Elijah, while he was full of zeal for the Torah, was taken up into heaven. Ananias and Azarias and Misael by believing, were delivered out of the flame. Daniel in his innocence was delivered out of the mouth of the lions. And thus consider through all generations that none that trust in him fail in strength. And fear not the words of a sinful man, for his glory is dung, and worms. Today he is lifted up, and tomorrow he shall not be found, because he is returned into his earth and his thought is come to nothing. You therefore, my sons, take courage, and behave manfully in the Torah, for by it you shall be glorious. And behold, I know that your brother Simon is a man of counsel; give ear to him always, and he shall be a father to you. And Judah Machabeus who is valiant and strong from his youth up, let him be the leader of your army, and he shall manage the war of the people. And you shall take to you all that observe the Torah, and revenge the wrong of your people. Render to the Gentiles their reward, and take heed to the precepts of the Torah.

And he blessed them, and was joined to his fathers. And he died in the hundred and forty-sixth year and he was buried by his sons in the sepulchers of his fathers in Modin, and all Israel mourned for him with great mourning.

Chapter 3

Judah and His Early Victories.
Then his son Judah, called Machabeus, rose up in his stead. And all his brethren helped him, and all they that had joined themselves to his father, and they fought with cheerfulness the battle of Israel. And he got his people great honor, and put on a breastplate as a giant, and girt his warlike armor about him in battles, and protected the camp with his sword. In his acts he was like a lion, and like a lion's whelp roaring for his prey. He pursued the wicked and sought them out, and them that troubled his people he burnt with fire. And his enemies were driven away for fear of him, and all the workers of iniquity were troubled and salvation prospered in his hand. And he grieved many kings, and made Jacob glad with his works, and his memory is blessed for ever. He went through the cities of Judea and destroyed the wicked out of them, and turned away wrath from Israel. He was renowned even to the utmost part of the earth, and he gathered them that were perishing. And Apollonius gathered together the Gentiles, and a numerous and great army from Samaria, to make war against Israel. And Judah understood it and went forth to meet him, and he overthrew him and killed him, and many fell down slain, and the rest fled away. And he took their spoils, and Judah took the sword of Apollonius, and fought with it all his lifetime.

And Seron captain of the army of Syria heard that Judah had assembled a company of the faithful, and a congregation with him, and he said, "I will get me a name, and will be glorified in the kingdom, and will overthrow Judah, and those that are with him, that have despised the edict of the king." He made himself ready, and the host of the wicked went up with him, strong succors, to be revenged of the children of Israel. And they approached even as far as Bethoron, and Judah went forth to meet him with a small company. But when they saw the army coming to meet them, they said to Judah, "How shall we, being few, be able to fight against so great a multitude and so strong, and we are ready to faint with fasting today?" And Judah said:

> It is an easy matter for many to be shut up in the hands of a few, and there is no difference in the sight of the God of heaven to deliver with a great multitude, or with a small company. For the success of war is not in the multitude of the army, but strength comes from heaven. They come against us with an insolent multitude, and with pride, to destroy us and our wives and our children, and to take our spoils. But we will fight for our lives and our laws, and the Lord himself will overthrow them before our face, but as for you, fear them not.

As soon as he had made an end of speaking, he rushed suddenly upon them, and Seron and his host were overthrown before him, and he pursued him by the descent of Bethoron even to the plain, and there fell of them eight hundred men, and the rest fled into the land of the Philistines. And the fear of Judah and of his brethren, and the dread of them fell upon all the nations round about them. And his fame came to the king, and all nations told of the battles of Judah.

The King's Strategy.
Now when King Antiochus heard these words, he was angry in his mind, and he sent and gathered the forces of all his kingdom, an exceeding strong army. He opened his treasury and gave out pay to the army for a year, and he commanded them, that they should be ready for all things. And he perceived that the money of his treasures failed, and that the tributes of the country were small because of the dissension, and the evil that he had brought upon the land, that he might take away the laws of old times. And he feared that he should not have as formerly enough for charges and gifts, which he had given before with a liberal hand, for he had abounded more than the kings that had been before him. And he was greatly perplexed in mind, and purposed to go into Persia, and to take tributes of the countries, and to gather much money. And he left Lysias, a nobleman of the blood royal, to oversee the affairs of the kingdom, from the river Euphrates even to the river of Egypt, and to bring up his son Antiochus, till he came again.

And he delivered to him half the army and the elephants, and he gave him charge concerning all that he would have done. And concerning the inhabitants of Judea and Jerusalem, that he should send an army against them to destroy and root out the strength of Israel and the remnant of Jerusalem, and to take away the memory of them from that place, and that he should settle strangers to dwell in all their coasts, and divide their land by lot. So the king took the half of the army that remained, and went forth from Antioch the chief city of his kingdom, in the hundred and forty-seventh year, and he passed over the river Euphrates, and went through the higher countries.

Preparations for Battle.

Then Lysias chose Ptolemy, the son of Dorymenus, and Nicanor, and Gorgias, mighty men of the king's friends. And he sent with them forty thousand men, and seven thousand horsemen to go into the land of Judea, and to destroy it according to the king's orders. So they went forth with all their power, and came, and pitched near Emmaus in the plain country. And the merchants of the countries heard the fame of them, and they took silver and gold in abundance, and servants, and they came into the camp to buy the children of Israel for slaves, and there were joined to them the forces of Syria, and of the land of the strangers.

And Judah and his brethren saw that evils were multiplied, and that the armies approached to their borders, and they knew the orders the king had given to destroy the people and utterly abolish them. And they said every man to his neighbor, "Let us raise up the low condition of our people, and let us fight for our people, and our sanctuary." And the assembly was gathered that they might be ready for battle, and that they might pray, and ask mercy and compassion.

Now Jerusalem was not inhabited, but was like a desert. There was none of her children that went in or out, and the sanctuary was trodden down. The children of strangers were in the citadel—there was the habitation of the Gentiles—and joy was taken away from Jacob. And the pipe and harp ceased there. They assembled together, and came to Maspha over against Jerusalem, for in Maspha was a place of prayer heretofore in Israel. They fasted that day, and put on haircloth, and put ashes upon their heads, they rent their garments and they laid open the books of the Torah, in which the Gentiles searched for the likeness of their idols. They brought the priestly ornaments, and the firstfruits and tithes, and stirred up the Nazarites that had fulfilled their days. And they cried with a loud voice toward heaven, saying, "What shall we do with these, and where shall we carry them? For your holies are trodden down, and are profaned, and your priests are in mourning, and are brought low. And behold the nations are come together against us to destroy us. You know what they intend against us. How shall we be able to stand before their face, unless you, O God, help us?" Then they sounded with trumpets, and cried out with a loud voice.

And after this Judah appointed captains over the people, over thousands, and over hundreds, and over fifties, and over tens. And he said to them that were building houses, or had betrothed wives, or were planting vineyards, or were fearful, that they should return every man to his house, according to the Torah. So they removed the camp, and pitched on the south side of Emmaus. And Judah said, "Gird yourselves, and be valiant men, and be ready in the morning, that you may fight with these nations that are assembled against us to destroy us and our sanctuary. For it is better for us to die in battle, than to see the evils of our nation, and of the holies. Nevertheless as it shall be the will of God in heaven so be it done."

Chapter 4

Victory over Gorgias.

Then Gorgias took five thousand men, and a thousand of the best horsemen, and they removed out of the camp by night so they might come upon the camp of the Jews and strike them suddenly. And the men that were of the citadel were their guides. And Judah heard of it, and rose up, he and the valiant men, to attack the king's forces that were in Emmaus. For as yet the army was dispersed from the camp. And Gorgias came by night into the camp of Judah, and found no man, and he sought them in the mountains, for he said, "These men flee from us." And when it was day, Judah shewed himself in the plain with three thousand men only, who neither had armor nor swords. And they saw the camp of the Gentiles that it was strong, and the men in breastplates, and the horsemen round about them, and these were trained up to war. And Judah said to the men that were with him, "Fear not their multitude, neither be afraid of their assault. Remember in what manner our fathers were saved in the Red Sea, when Pharaoh pursued them with a great army. And now let us cry to heaven and the Lord will have mercy on us, and will remember the covenant of our fathers, and will destroy this army before our face this day. And all nations shall know that there is one that redeems and delivers Israel." The strangers lifted up their eyes, and saw them coming against them. They went out of the camp to battle, and they that were with Judah sounded the trumpet. And they joined the battle, and the Gentiles were routed and fled into the plain. But all the hindmost of them fell by the sword, and they pursued them as far as Gezeron, and even to the plains of Idumea, and of Azotus, and of Jamnia, and there fell of them to the number of three thousand men. Judah returned again with his army that followed him, and said to the people, "Be not greedy of the spoils, for there is war before us. And Gorgias and his army are near us in the mountain, but stand now against our enemies, and overthrow them, and you shall take the spoils afterwards with safety." And as Judah was speaking these words, behold part of them appeared looking forth from the mountain. And Gorgias saw that his men were put to flight, and that they had set fire to the camp, for the smoke that was seen declared what was done. And when they had seen this, they were seized with great fear, seeing at the same time Judah and his army in the plain ready to fight. So they all fled away into the land of the strangers. And Judah returned to take the spoils of the camp, and they got much gold, and silver, and blue silk, and purple of the sea, and great riches. And returning home they sung a hymn, and blessed God in heaven, because he is good, because his mercy endures for ever. So Israel had a great deliverance that day.

Victory over Lysias.

And such of the strangers as escaped, went and told Lysias all that had happened. And when he heard these things, he was amazed and discouraged, because things had not succeeded in Israel according to his mind, and as the king had commanded. So the year following Lysias gathered together threescore thousand chosen men, and five thousand horsemen, that he might subdue them. And they came into Judea, and pitched their tents in Bethoron, and Judah met them with ten thousand men. And they saw that the army was strong, and he prayed, and said:

> Blessed are you, O Savior of Israel, who broke the violence of the mighty by the hand of your servant David, and delivered up the camp of the strangers into the hands of Jonathan the son of Saul and of his armor bearer. Shut up this army in the hands of your people Israel, and let them be confounded in their host and their horsemen. Strike them with fear, and cause the boldness of their strength to languish, and let them quake at their own destruction. Cast them down with the sword of them that love you, and let all that know your name, praise you with hymns.

They joined battle, and there fell of the army of Lysias five thousand men. When Lysias saw that his men were put to flight, and how bold the Jews were, and that they were ready either to live, or to die manfully, he went to Antioch, and chose soldiers, that they might come again into Judea with greater numbers.

Purification and Rededication of the Temple.
Then Judah and his brethren said, "Behold our enemies are discomfited. Let us go up now to cleanse the holy places and to repair them." And all the army assembled together, and they went up into mount Zion. They saw the sanctuary desolate, and the altar profaned, and the gates burnt, and shrubs growing up in the courts as in a forest, or on the mountains, and the chambers joining to the Temple thrown down. And they rent their garments, and made great lamentation, and put ashes on their heads, and they fell face down to the ground on their faces, and they sounded with the trumpets of alarm, and they cried towards heaven. Then Judah appointed men to fight against them that were in the citadel, till they had cleansed the holy places. And he chose priests without blemish, whose will was set upon the Torah of God. And they cleansed the holy places, and took away the stones that had been defiled into an unclean place. And he considered about the altar of burnt offerings that had been profaned, what he should do with it. And a good counsel came into their minds, to pull it down, lest it should be a reproach to them, because the Gentiles had defiled it; so they threw it down. And they laid up the stones in the mountain of the Temple in a convenient place, till there should come a prophet, and give answer concerning them. Then they took whole stones according to the Torah, and built a new altar according to the former. And they built up the holy places, and the things that were within the Temple and they sanctified the Temple, and the courts. And they made new holy vessels, and brought in the candlestick, the altar of incense, and the table into the Temple. And they put incense upon the altar, and lighted up the lamps that were upon the candlestick, and they gave light in the Temple. And they set the loaves upon the table, and hung up the veils, and finished all the works that they had begun to make. And they arose before the morning on the twenty-fifth day of the ninth month (which is the month of Kislev) in the hundred and forty-eighth year. And they offered sacrifice according to the Torah upon the new altar of burnt offerings which they had made. According to the time, and according to the day wherein the heathens had defiled it, in the same was it dedicated anew with canticles, and harps, and lutes, and cymbals. And all the people fell upon their faces, and adored, and blessed up to heaven, him that had prospered them. And they kept the dedication of the altar eight days, and they offered burnt offerings with joy, and sacrifices of salvation, and of praise. And they adorned the front of the Temple with crowns of gold and escutcheons, and they renewed the gates and the chambers, and hung doors upon them. And there was exceeding great joy among the people, and the reproach of the Gentiles was turned away. And Judah, and his brethren, and all the church of Israel decreed, that the day of the dedication of the altar should be kept in its season from year to year for eight days, from the twenty-fifth day of the month of Kislev, with

joy and gladness. They built up also at that time mount Zion, with high walls and strong towers round about, lest the Gentiles should at any time come and tread it down as they did before. And he placed a garrison there to keep it, and he fortified it to secure Bethsura, that the people might have a defense against Idumea.

Chapter 5

Victories over Hostile Neighbors.

Now it came to pass, when the nations round about heard that the altar and the sanctuary were built up as before, that they were exceedingly angry. And they thought to destroy the generation of Jacob that were among them, and they began to kill some of the people, and to persecute them. Then Judah fought against the children of Esau in Idumea, and them that were in Acrabathane, because they beset the Israelites round about, and he made a great slaughter of them. And he remembered the malice of the children of Bean, who were a snare and a stumbling block to the people by lying in wait for them in the way. And they were shut up by him in towers, and he set upon them, and devoted them to utter destruction, and burnt their towers with fire, and all that were in them. Then he passed over to the children of Ammon, where he found a mighty power, and much people, and Timotheus was their captain. And he fought many battles with them, and they were discomfited in their sight, and he smote them. And he took the city of Gazer and her towns, and returned into Judea.

Liberation of Jews in Galilee and Gilead.

And the Gentiles that were in Gilead assembled themselves together against the Israelites that were in their quarters to destroy them, and they fled into the fortress of Datheman. And they sent letters to Judah and his brethren, saying:

> The heathens that are round about are gathered together against us, to destroy us. And they are preparing to come and to take the fortress into which we are fled, and Timotheus is the captain of their host. Now therefore come and deliver us out of their hands, for many of us are slain. And all our brethren that were in the places of Tubin are killed, and they have carried away their wives, and their children, captives, and taken their spoils, and they have slain there almost a thousand men.

And while they were yet reading these letters, behold there came other messengers out of Galilee with their garments rent, who related according to these words, saying that they of Ptolemais and of Tyre and of Sidon were assembled against them, and all Galilee is filled with strangers, in order to consume us.

Now when Judah and all the people heard these words, a great assembly met together to consider what they should do for their brethren that were in trouble, and were assaulted by them. And Judah said to Simon his brother, "Choose men, and go, and deliver your brethren in Galilee. And I, and my brother Jonathan, will go into the country of Gilead." And he left Joseph the son of Zacharias, and Azarias, captain of the people, with the remnant of the army in Judea to keep it. And he commanded them, saying, "Take the charge of this people, but make no war against the heathens, till we return." Now three thousand men were allotted to Simon to go into Galilee, and eight thousand to Judah to go into the land of Gilead. And Simon went into Galilee, and fought many battles with the heathens, and the heathens were discomfited before his face, and he pursued them even to the gate of Ptolemais. There fell of the heathens almost three thousand men, and he took the spoils of them, and he took with him those that were in Galilee and in Arbatis with their wives, and children, and all that they had, and he brought them into Judea with great joy. And Judah Machabeus and Jonathan his brother passed over the Jordan and went three days journey through the desert. And the Nabutheans met them and received them in a peaceable manner, and told them all that happened to their brethren in the land of Gilead, and that many of them were shut up in Barasa, and in Bosor, and in Alima, and in Casphor, and in Mageth, and in Carnaim: all these strong and great cities. Yea, and that they were kept shut up in the rest of the cities of Gilead, and that they had appointed to bring their army on the morrow near to these cities, and to take them and to destroy them all in one day. Then Judah and his army suddenly turned their march into the desert, to Bosor, and took the city, and he slew every male by the edge of the sword, and took all their spoils, and burnt it with fire. And they left from there by night, and went till they came to the fortress. And it came to pass that early in the morning, when they lifted up their eyes, behold there were people without number, carrying ladders and engines to take the fortress and assault them. Judah saw that the fight was begun, and the cry of the battle went up to heaven like a trumpet, and a great cry out of the city. And he said to his host, "Fight today for your brethren." He came with three companies behind them, and they sounded their trumpets, and cried out in prayer. The host of Timotheus understood that it was Machabeus, and they fled away before his face, and they made a great slaughter of them, and there fell of them in that day almost eight thousand men. And Judah turned aside to Maspha, and assaulted, and took it, and he slew every male thereof, and took the spoils thereof, and burnt it with fire. From thence he marched, and took Casbon, and Mageth, and Bosor, and the rest of the cities of Gilead. But after this Timotheus gathered another army, and camped over against Raphon beyond the torrent. Judah sent men to view the army, and they brought him word, saying, "All the nations that are round about us are assembled unto him an army exceedingly great. And they have hired the Arabians to help them, and they have pitched their tents beyond the torrent, ready to come to fight against you." And Judah went to meet them. And Timotheus said to the captains of his army, "When Judah and his army come near the torrent of water, if he pass over unto us first, we shall not be able to withstand him, for he will certainly prevail over us. But if he be afraid to pass over, and camp on the other side of the river, we will pass over to them and shall prevail against him." Now when Judah came near the torrent of water, he set the scribes of the people by the torrent, and commanded them, saying, "Suffer no man to stay behind, but let all come to the battle." And he passed over to them first, and all the people after him, and all the heathens were discomfited before them, and they threw away their weapons and fled to the temple that was in Carnaim. And he took that city, and the temple he burnt with fire, with all things that were therein, and Carnaim was subdued, and could not stand against the face of Judah.

Return to Jerusalem.
And Judah gathered together all the Israelites that were in the land of Gilead, from the least even to the greatest, and their wives, and children, and an army exceedingly great, to come into the land of Judea. And they came as far as Ephron. Now this was a great city situated in the way, strongly fortified, and there was no means to turn from it on the right hand or on the left, but the way was through the midst of it. They that were in the city shut themselves in, and stopped up the gates with stones, and Judah sent to them with peaceable words, saying, "Let us pass through your land, to go into our country and no man shall hurt you. We will only pass through on foot." But they would not open to them. Then Judah commanded proclamation to be made in the camp, that they should make an assault every man in the place where he was. And the men of the army drew near, and he assaulted that city all the day and all the night, and the city was delivered into his hands. And they slew every male with the edge of the sword, and he razed the city, and took the spoils thereof, and passed through all the city over them that were slain. Then they passed over the Jordan to the great plain that is over against Bethsan. And Judah gathered together the hindmost, and he exhorted the people all the way through, till they came into the land of Judea. And they went up to mount Zion with joy and gladness, and offered burnt offerings, because not one of them was slain, till they had returned in peace.

Joseph and Azariah Defeated.
  Now in the days that Judah and Jonathan were in the land of Gilead, and Simon his brother in Galilee before Ptolemais, Joseph the son of Zacharias, and Azarias captain of the soldiers, heard of the good success, and the battles that were fought. And he said, "Let us also get us a name, and let us go fight against the Gentiles that are round about us." And he gave charge to them that were in his army, and they went towards Jamnia. And Gorgias and his men went out of the city to give them battle. And Joseph and Azarias were put to flight, and were pursued unto the borders of Judea. And there fell on that day of the people of Israel about two thousand men, and there was a great overthrow of the people, because they did not hearken to Judah, and his brethren, thinking that they should do manfully. But they were not of the seed of those men by whom salvation was brought to Israel.

Victories at Hebron and Azotus.
  And the men of Judea were magnified exceedingly in the sight of all Israel, and of all the nations where their name was heard. And people assembled to them with joyful acclamations. Then Judah and his brethren went forth and attacked the children of Esau in the land toward the south, and he took Hebron and her towns, and he burnt the walls thereof and the towers all round it. And he removed his camp to go into the land of the aliens, and he went through Samaria. In that day some priests fell in battle, while desiring to do manfully they went out unadvisedly to fight. And Judah turned to Azotus into the land of the strangers, and he threw down their altars, and he burnt the statues of their gods with fire, and he took the spoils of the cities, and returned into the land of Judea.

CHAPTER 6

  Now King Antiochus was going through the higher countries, and he heard that the city of Elymais in Persia was greatly renowned, and abounding in silver and gold. And that there was in it a temple, exceedingly rich, and coverings of gold, and breastplates, and shields which King Alexander, son of Philip the Macedonian that reigned first in Greece, had left there. Lo, he came, and sought to take the city and to pillage it. But he was not able, because the design was known to them that were in the city. And they rose up against him in battle, and he fled away from there, and departed with great sadness, and returned towards Babylonia. And while he was in Persia, there came one that told him how the armies that were in the land of Judea were put to flight, and that Lysias went with a very great power, and was put to flight before the face of the Jews, and that they were grown strong by the armor, and power, and store of spoils, which they had gotten out of the camps which they had destroyed. And that they had thrown down the abomination which he had set up upon the altar in Jerusalem, and that they had compassed about the sanctuary with high walls as before, and Bethsura also his city. And it came to pass when the king heard these words, that he was struck with fear, and exceedingly moved, and he laid himself down upon his bed, and fell sick for grief, because it had not fallen out to him as he imagined. And he remained there many days for great grief came more and more and more upon him, and he made account that he should die. And he called for all his friends, and said to them:

> Sleep is gone from my eyes, and I am fallen away, and my heart is cast down for anxiety. And I said in my heart, "Into how much tribulation am I come, and into what floods of sorrow, wherein now I am. I that was pleasant and beloved in my power! But now I remember the evils that I have done in Jerusalem, from where also I took away all the spoils of gold, and of silver that were in it, and I sent to destroy the inhabitants of Judea without cause. I know therefore that for this cause these evils have found me, and behold I perish with great grief in a strange land."

Then he called Philip, one of his friends, and he made him regent over all his kingdom. And he gave him the crown, and his robe, and his ring, that he should go to Antiochus his son, and should bring him up for the kingdom. So King Antiochus died there in the year one hundred and forty-nine. And Lysias understood that the king was dead, and he set up Antiochus his son to reign, whom he brought up young, and he called his name Eupator.

Siege of the Citadel.

Now they that were in the citadel had shut up the Israelites round about the holy places, and they were continually seeking their hurt, and to strengthen the Gentiles. And Judah purposed to destroy them, and he called together all the people, to besiege them. And they came together and besieged them in the year one hundred and fifty, and they made battering slings and engines. And some of the besieged got out, and some wicked men of Israel joined themselves unto them. And they went to the king, and said:

> How long do you delay to execute the judgment, and to revenge our brethren? We determined to serve your father and to do according to his orders, and obey his edicts. And for this they of our nation are alienated from us, and have slain as many of us as they could find, and have spoiled our inheritances. Neither have they put forth their hand against us only, but also against all our borders. And behold they have approached this day to the citadel of Jerusalem to take it, and they

have fortified the stronghold of Bethsura. And unless you speedily prevent them, they will do greater things than these, and you shall not be able to subdue them.

Now when the king heard this, he was angry, and he called together all his friends and the captains of his army and them that were over the horsemen. There came also to him hired troops from other realms and from the islands of the sea. And the number of his army was an hundred thousand footmen, twenty thousand horsemen, and thirty-two elephants, trained to battle. And they went through Idumea and approached to Bethsura and fought many days, and they made engines but they sallied forth and burnt them with fire, and fought manfully.

Battle of Beth-Zechariah.

And Judah departed from the citadel, and removed the camp to Beth-Zechariah, over against the king's camp. And the king rose before it was light, and made his troops march on fiercely towards the way of Beth-Zechariah, and the armies made themselves ready for the battle, and they sounded the trumpets. And they showed the elephants the blood of grapes and mulberries to provoke them to fight. They distributed the beasts by the legions and there stood by every elephant a thousand men in coats of mail, with helmets of brass on their heads and five hundred horsemen set in order were chosen for every beast. Wherever the beast was, they were there, and wherever it went, they went, and they departed not from it. And upon the beast, were strong wooden towers which covered every one of them, and engines upon them. And upon every tower were thirty-two valiant men, who fought from above, and an Indian to rule the beast. And the rest of the horsemen he placed on this side and on that side at the two wings, with trumpets to stir up the army, and to hasten them forward that stood thick together in the legions thereof. Now when the sun shone upon the shields of gold, and of brass, the mountains glittered, and they shone like lamps of fire. And part of the king's army was distinguished by the high mountains, and the other part by the low places, and they marched on warily and orderly. And all the inhabitants of the land were moved at the noise of their multitude, and the marching of the company, and the rattling of the armor, for the army was exceedingly great and strong. And Judah and his army drew near for battle, and there fell of the king's army six hundred men. And Eleazar the son of Saura saw one of the beasts harnessed with the king's harness, and it was higher than the other beasts, and it seemed to him that the king was on it. And he exposed himself to deliver his people and to get himself an everlasting name. And he ran up to it boldly in the midst of the legion, killing on the right hand, and on the left, and they fell by him on this side and that side. He went between the feet of the elephant, and put himself under it, and slew it. And it fell to the ground upon him, and he died there. Then seeing the strength of the king and the fierceness of his army, they turned away from them.

The Siege of Jerusalem.

But the king's army went up against them to Jerusalem and pitched their tents against Judea and Mount Zion. He made peace with them that were in Bethsura, and they came forth out of the city, because they had no provisions, being shut up there, for it was the year of rest to the land. And the king took Bethsura and placed there a garrison to keep it. He turned his army against the sanctuary for many days and set up there battering slings, and engines and instruments to cast fire, and engines to cast stones and javelins, and pieces to shoot arrows, and slings. And they also made engines against their engines, and they fought for many days. But there were no provisions in the city, because it was the seventh year, and such as had stayed in Judea of them that came from among the nations, had eaten the residue of all that which had been stored up. And there remained in the holy places but a few, for the famine had prevailed over them, and they were dispersed every man to his own place.

Peace Treaty.

Now Lysias heard that Philip, whom King Antiochus while he lived had appointed to bring up his son Antiochus, and to reign to be king, was returned from Persia and Media with the army that went with him and that he sought to take upon him the affairs of the kingdom. Wherefore he made haste to go and say to the king and to the captains of the army, "We decay daily, and our provisions are small, and the place that we lay siege to is strong, and it lies upon us to take order for the affairs of the kingdom. Now therefore let us come to an agreement with these men, and make peace with them and with all their nation. And let us covenant with them, that they may live according to their own laws as before. For because of our despising their laws, they have been provoked, and have done all these things." And the proposal was acceptable in the sight of the king and of the princes, and he sent to them to make peace, and they accepted of it. And the king and the princes swore to them, and they came out of the stronghold. Then the king entered into Mount Zion and saw the strength of the place, and he quickly broke the oath that he had taken and gave commandment to throw down the wall round about. And he departed in haste and returned to Antioch, where he found Philip master of the city, and he fought against him and took the city.

Chapter 7

Expedition of Bacchides and Alcimus.

In the hundred and fifty-first year Demetrius the son of Seleucus departed from the city of Rome, and came up with a few men into a city of the sea coast, and reigned there. And it came to pass, as he entered into the house of the kingdom of his fathers, that the army seized upon Antiochus, and Lysias, to bring them unto him. And when he knew it, he said, "Let me not see their face." So the army slew them. And Demetrius sat upon the throne of his kingdom. And there came to him the wicked and ungodly men of Israel. And Alcimus was at the head of them, who desired to be made high priest. And they accused the people to the king, saying, "Judah and his brethren have destroyed all your friends, and he has driven us out of our land. Now therefore send some man whom you trust, and let him go, and see all the havoc he has made amongst us, and in the king's lands. And let him punish all his friends and their helpers."

Then the king chose Bacchides, one of his friends that ruled beyond the great river in the kingdom, and was faithful to the king. And he sent him to see the havoc that Judah had made, and the wicked Alcimus he made high priest, and commanded him to take revenge upon the children of Israel. And they arose, and came with a great army into the land of Judea, and they sent messengers, and spoke to Judah and his brethren with peaceable words deceitfully. But they gave no heed to their words, for they saw that they were coming with a great army. Then there assembled to Alcimus and Bacchides a company of the scribes to require things that are just, and first the Assideans that were among the children of Israel, and they sought peace of them. For they said, "One that is a priest of the seed of Aaron is come, he will not deceive us." And he spoke to them peaceably and he swore to them, saying, "We will do you no harm nor your friends." And they believed him. And he took threescore of them, and slew them in one day, according to the word that is written, "The flesh of your saints, and the blood of them they have shed round about Jerusalem, and there was none to bury them."

Then fear and trembling fell upon all the people, for they said, "There is no truth, nor justice among them, for they have broken the covenant and the oath which they made." And Bacchides removed the camp from Jerusalem, and pitched in Bethzecha, and he sent, and took many of them that were fled away from him, and some of the people he killed, and threw them into a great pit. Then he committed the country to Alcimus, and left with him troops to help him. So Bacchides went away to the king, but Alcimus did what he could to maintain his chief priesthood. And they that disturbed the people resorted to him, and they got the land of Judea into their power, and did much hurt in Israel. And Judah saw all the evils that Alcimus, and they that were with him, did to the children of Israel, much more than the Gentiles. And he went out into all the coasts of Judea round about, and took vengeance upon the men that had revolted, and they ceased to go forth any more into the country. And Alcimus saw that Judah and they that were with him prevailed, and he knew that he could not stand against them, and he went back to the king and accused them of many crimes.

Defeat of Nicanor.
And the king sent Nicanor, one of his principal lords, who was a great enemy to Israel, and he commanded him to destroy the people. Nicanor came to Jerusalem with a great army, and he sent to Judah and to his brethren deceitfully with friendly words, saying, "Let there be no fighting between me and you. I will come with a few men to see your faces with peace." And he came to Judah, and they saluted one another peaceably, and the enemies were prepared to take away Judah by force. And the thing was known to Judah that he was come to him with deceit, and he was much afraid of him, and would not see his face any more. And Nicanor knew that his counsel was discovered, and he went out to fight against Judah near Capharsalama. And there fell of Nicanor's army almost five thousand men, and they fled into the city of David. After this, Nicanor went up into Mount Zion, and some of the priests and the people came out to salute him peaceably and show him the burnt offerings that were offered for the king. But he mocked them and despised them, and abused them, and he spoke proudly and swore in anger, saying, "Unless Judah and his army be delivered into my hands, as soon as ever I return in peace, I will burn this house." And he went out in a great rage. And the priests went in and stood before the face of the altar and the Temple, and weeping, they said, "You, O Lord, have chosen this house for your name to be called upon therein, that it might be a house of prayer and supplication for your people. Be avenged of this man, and his army, and let them fall by the sword. Remember their blasphemies and suffer them not to continue any longer." Then Nicanor went out from Jerusalem and encamped near to Bethoron, and an army of Syria joined him. But Judah pitched in Adarsa with three thousand men and prayed, and said, "O Lord, when they that were sent by King Sennacherib blasphemed you, an angel went out and slew of them a hundred and eighty-five thousand. Even so destroy this army in our sight today, and let the rest know that he has spoken ill against your sanctuary, and judge him according to his wickedness." And the armies joined battle on the thirteenth day of the month Adar, and the army of Nicanor was defeated, and he himself was first slain in the battle. And when his army saw that Nicanor was slain, they threw away their weapons and fled. And they pursued after them

one day's journey from Adazer, even till they come to Gazara, and they sounded the trumpets after them with signals. And they went forth out of all the towns of Judea round about, and they pushed them with the horns, and they turned again to them, and they were all slain with the sword, and there was not left of them so much as one. And they took the spoils of them for a booty, and they cut off Nicanor's head, and his right hand, which he had proudly stretched out, and they brought it and hung it up over against Jerusalem. And the people rejoiced exceedingly, and they spent that day with great joy. And he ordained that this day should be kept every year, being the thirteenth of the month of Adar. And the land of Judea was quiet for a short time.

Chapter 8

Eulogy of the Romans.

Now Judah heard of the fame of the Romans, that they are powerful and strong, and willingly agree to all things that are requested of them, and that whosoever have come to them, they have made amity with them, and that they are mighty in power. And they heard of their battles, and their noble acts, which they had done in Galatia, how they conquered them and brought them under tribute, and how great things they had done in the land of Spain, and that they had brought under their power the mines of silver and of gold that are there, and had gotten possession of all the place by their counsel and patience, and had conquered places that were very far off from them, and kings that came against them from the ends of the earth, and had overthrown them with great slaughter, and the rest pay them tribute every year. And that they had defeated in battle Philip, and Perses the king of the Ceteans, and the rest that had borne arms against them, and had conquered them. And how Antiochus the great king of Asia, who went to fight against them, having a hundred and twenty elephants, with horsemen and chariots and a very great army, was routed by them, and how they took him alive and appointed to him that both he and they that should reign after him should pay a great tribute, and that he should give hostages, and that which was agreed upon. And the country of the Indians, and of the Medes, and of the Lydians, some of their best provinces, and those which they had taken from them they gave to King Eumenes. And that they who were in Greece had a mind to go and destroy them, and they had knowledge thereof, and they sent a general against them, and fought with them, and many of them were slain, and they carried away their wives and their children captives, and spoiled them, and took possession of their land, and threw down their walls, and brought them to be their servants unto this day. And the other kingdoms and islands, that at any time had resisted them, they had destroyed and brought under their power.

But with their friends, and such as relied upon them, they kept amity, and had conquered kingdoms that were near, and that were far off. For all that heard their name were afraid of them. That whom they had a mind to help to a kingdom, those reigned, and whom they would, they deposed from a kingdom, and they were greatly exalted. And none of all these wore a crown, or was clothed in purple, to be magnified thereby. And that they made themselves a senate house and consulted daily three hundred and twenty men that sat in council always for the people, that they might do the things that were right. And that they committed their government to one man every year, to rule over all their country, and they all obey one, and there is no envy, nor jealousy amongst them.

Treaty with the Romans.
So Judah chose Eupolemus the son of John, the son of Jacob, and Jason the son of Eleazar, and he sent them to Rome to make a league of amity and confederacy with them. And that they might take off from them the yoke of the Grecians, for they saw that they oppressed the kingdom of Israel with servitude. And they went to Rome, a very long journey, and they entered into the senate house, and said, "Judah Machabeus, and his brethren, and the people of the Jews have sent us to you, to make alliance and peace with you, and that we may be registered your confederates and friends." And the proposal was pleasing in their sight. And this is the copy of the writing that they wrote back again, graven in tables of brass, and sent to Jerusalem, that it might be with them there for a memorial of the peace and alliance:

> Good success be to the Romans, and to the people of the Jews, by sea and by land for ever, and far be the sword and enemy from them. But if there come first any war upon the Romans, or any of their confederates, in all their dominions, the nation of the Jews shall help them according as the time shall direct, with all their heart. Neither shall they give them, while they are fighting, or furnish them with wheat, or arms, or money, or ships, as it has seemed good to the Romans, and they shall obey their orders, without taking any thing of them. In like manner also if war shall come first upon the nation of the Jews, the Romans shall help them with all their heart, according as the time shall permit them. And there shall not be given to them that come to their aid, either wheat, or arms, or money, or ships, as it has seemed good to the Romans, and they shall observe their orders without deceit. According to these articles did the Romans covenant with the people of the Jews. And if after this one party or the other shall have a mind to add to these articles, or take away anything, they may do it at their pleasure, and whatsoever they shall add, or take away, shall be ratified. Moreover concerning the evils that Demetrius the king has done against them, we have written to him,

saying, "Why have you made your yoke heavy upon our friends, and allies, the Jews?" If therefore they come again to us complaining of you, we will do them justice, and will make war against you by sea and land.

Chapter 9

Death of Judah.

In the meantime, when Demetrius heard that Nicanor and his army were fallen in battle, he sent again Bacchides and Alcimus into Judea, and the right wing of his army with them. And they took the road that lead to Galgal, and they camped in Masaloth, which is in Arabella, and they made themselves masters of it, and slew many people. In the first month of the hundred and fifty-second year they brought the army to Jerusalem. And they arose, and went to Berea with twenty thousand men, and two thousand horsemen. Now Judah had pitched his tents in Laisa, and three thousand chosen men with him. They saw the multitude of the army that they were many, and they were seized with great fear and many withdrew themselves out of the camp, and there remained of them no more than eight hundred men. And Judah saw that his army slipped away, and the battle pressed upon him, and his heart was cast down because he had not time to gather them together, and he was discouraged. Then he said to them that remained, "Let us arise, and go against our enemies, if we may be able to fight against them." But they dissuaded him, saying, "We shall not be able, but let us save our lives now, and return to our brethren, and then we will fight against them, for we are but few." Then Judah said, "God forbid we should do this thing, and flee away from them, but if our time be come, let us die manfully for our brethren, and let us not stain our glory." And the army removed out of the camp and stood over against them, and the horsemen were divided into two troops, and the slingers, and the archers went before the army, and they that were in the front were all men of valor. And Bacchides was in the right wing, and the legion drew near on two sides, and they sounded the trumpets. And they also were on Judah's side, even they also cried out, and the earth shook at the noise of the armies, and the battle was fought from morning even unto the evening. And Judah perceived that the stronger part of the army of Bacchides was on the right side, and all the stout of heart came together with him. And the right wing was discomfited by them, and he pursued them even to the Mount Azotus. And they that were in the left wing saw that the right wing was discomfited, and they followed after Judah, and them that were with him, at their back. And the battle was hard fought, and there fell many wounded of the one side and of the other. And Judah was slain, and the rest fled away. And Jonathan and

Simon took Judah their brother, and buried him in the sepulcher of their fathers in the city of Modin. And all the people of Israel bewailed him with great lamentation, and they mourned for him many days and said, "How is the mighty man fallen, that saved the people of Israel!" But the rest of the words of the wars of Judah and of the noble acts that he did, and of his greatness, are not written, for they were very many.

Jonathan Succeeds Judah.

And it came to pass after the death of Judah, that the wicked began to put forth their heads in all the confines of Israel, and all the workers of iniquity rose up. In those days there was a very great famine, and they and all their country yielded to Bacchides. And Bacchides chose the wicked men, and made them lords of the country. And they sought out, and made a diligent search after the friends of Judah, and brought them to Bacchides, and he took vengeance of them, and abused them. And there was a great tribulation in Israel, such as was not since the day that there was no prophet seen in Israel. And all the friends of Judah came together and said to Jonathan, "Since your brother Judah died, there is not a man like him to go forth against our enemies, Bacchides, and them that are the enemies of our nation. Now therefore we have chosen you this day to be our prince, and captain in his stead to fight our battles." So Jonathan took upon him the government at that time, and rose up in the place of Judah his brother.

Bacchides Pursues Jonathan.

And Bacchides had knowledge of it, and sought to kill him. And Jonathan and Simon his brother knew it, and all that were with them, and they fled into the desert of Thecua, and they pitched by the water of the lake of Asphar. And Bacchides understood it, and he came himself with all his army over the Jordan on the Sabbath day. And Jonathan sent his brother, a captain of the people, to desire the Nabutheans his friends, that they would lend them their equipage, which was copious. And the children of Jambri came forth out of Madaba, and took John, and all that he had, and went away with them. After this it was told Jonathan, and Simon his brother, that the children of Jambri made a great marriage and were bringing the bride out of Madaba, the daughter of one of the great princes of Chanaan, with great pomp. And they remembered the blood of John their brother, and they went up and hid themselves under the cover of the mountain. And they lifted up their eyes and saw a tumult and great preparation. And the bridegroom came forth, and his friends and his brethren to meet them with timbrels and musical instruments and many weapons. And they rose up against them from the place where they lay in ambush, and slew them, and there fell many wounded, and the rest fled into the mountains, and they took all their spoils. And the marriage was turned into mourning, and the noise of their musical instruments into lamentation. And they took revenge for the blood of their brother and returned to the bank of the Jordan.

And Bacchides heard it, and he came on the Sabbath day even to the bank of the Jordan with a great power. And Jonathan said to his company, "Let us arise, and fight against our enemies, for it is not now as yesterday, and the day before. And behold the battle is before us, and the water of the Jordan on this side and on that side, and banks, and marshes and woods, and there is no place for us to turn aside. Now therefore cry to heaven, that you may be delivered from the hand of your enemies." And they joined battle. And Jonathan stretched forth his hand to strike Bacchides, but he turned away from him backwards. And Jonathan and they that were with him leaped into the Jordan and swam over the Jordan to them. And there fell of Bacchides' side that day a thousand men, and they returned to Jerusalem. And they built strong cities in Judea, the fortress that was in Jericho, and in Ammaus, and in Bethoron, and in Bethel, and Thamnata, and Phara, and Thopo, with high walls, and gates, and bars. And he placed garrisons in them, that they might wage war against Israel. And he fortified the city of Bethsura, and Gazara, and the citadel, and set garrisons in them, and provisions. And he took the sons of the chief men of the country for hostages, and put them in the citadel in Jerusalem in custody.

Now in the year one hundred and fifty-three, the second month, Alcimus commanded the walls of the inner court of the sanctuary to be thrown down and the works of the prophets to be destroyed, and he began to destroy. At that time Alcimus was struck and his works were hindered, and his mouth was stopped, and he was taken with a palsy, so that he could no more speak a word, nor give order concerning his house. And Alcimus died at that time in great torment. And Bacchides saw that Alcimus was dead, and he returned to the king, and the land was quiet for two years. And all the wicked held a council, saying, "Behold Jonathan, and they that are with him, dwell at ease, and without fear. Now therefore let us bring Bacchides here, and he shall take them all in one night." So they went and gave him counsel. And he arose to come with a great army, and he sent letters secretly to his adherents that were in Judea, to seize upon Jonathan, and them that were with him, but they could not, for their design was known to them. And he apprehended of the men of the country, that were the principal authors of the mischief, fifty men, and slew them. Jonathan and Simon, and they that were with him, retired into Bethbessen, which is in the desert, and he repaired the breaches thereof, and they fortified it. And when Bacchides knew it, he gathered together all his multitude and sent word to them that were of Judea. He came and camped above Bethbessen, and fought against it many days, and made engines. But Jonathan left his brother Simon in the city, and went forth into the country and came with a number of men and struck Odares, and his brethren, and the children of Phaseron in their tents, and he began to slay, and to increase in forces. But Simon and they that were with him, sallied out of the city and burnt the engines. They fought against Bacchides and he was discomfited by them and they afflicted him exceedingly, for his counsel and his enterprise was in vain. And he was angry with the wicked men that had given him counsel to come into their country, and he slew many of them, and he purposed to return with the rest into their country. And Jonathan had knowledge of it, and he sent ambassadors to him to make peace with him, and to restore to him the prisoners. And he accepted it willingly, and did according to his words, and swore that he would do him no harm all the days of his life. And he restored to him the prisoners which he before had taken out of the land of Judea, and he returned and went away into his own country, and he came no more into their borders. So the sword ceased from Israel, and Jonathan dwelt in Machmas, and began there to judge the people, and he destroyed the wicked out of Israel.

CHAPTER 10

Jonathan Becomes High Priest.

Now in the hundred and sixtieth year Alexander the son of Antiochus, surnamed the Illustrious, came up and took Ptolemais, and they received him, and he reigned there. And King Demetrius heard of it, and gathered together an exceedingly great army, and went forth against him to fight. And Demetrius sent a letter to Jonathan with peaceable words, to magnify him. For he said, "Let us first make a peace with him, before he makes one with Alexander against us. For he will remember all the evils that we have done against him, and against his brother, and against his nation." And he gave him authority to gather together an army, and to make arms, and that he should be his confederate, and the hostages that were in the citadel, he commanded to be delivered to him. Jonathan came to Jerusalem and read the letters in the hearing of all the people, and of them that were in the citadel. And they were struck with great fear, because they heard that the king had given him authority to gather together an army. And the hostages were delivered to Jonathan, and he restored them to their parents. And Jonathan dwelt in Jerusalem, and began to build and repair the city. And he ordered workmen to build the walls, and Mount Zion round about with square stones for fortification. And so they did. The strangers that were in the strongholds, which Bacchides had built, fled away. And every man left his place and departed into his own country. Only in Bethsura there remained some of them that had forsaken the Torah and the commandments of God, for this was a place of refuge for them. King Alexander heard of the promises that Demetrius had made Jonathan, and they told him of the battles and the worthy acts that he and his brethren had done, and the labours that they had endured. And he said, "Shall we find such another man? Now therefore we will make him our friend and our confederate." So he wrote a letter and sent it to him according to these words, saying, "King Alexander to his brother Jonathan, greeting. We have heard of thee, that you are a man of great power, and fit to be our friend. Now therefore we make you this day high priest of your nation, and that you be called the king's friend, (and he sent him a purple robe and a crown of gold) and that you be of one mind with us in our affairs, and keep friendship with us." Then Jonathan put on the holy vestment in the seventh month, in the year one hundred and sixty, at the Feast of the Tabernacles, and he gathered together an army, and made a great number of arms.

A Letter from Demetrius to Jonathan.

And Demetrius heard these words and was exceedingly sorry, and said, "What is this that we have done, that Alexander has prevented us to gain the friendship of the Jews to strengthen himself? I also will write to them words of request, and offer dignities and gifts, that they may be with me to aid me." And he wrote to them in these words:

> King Demetrius to the nation of the Jews, greeting. Whereas you have kept covenant with us and have continued in our friendship, and have not joined with our enemies. We have heard of it and are glad. Wherefore now continue still to keep fidelity towards us, and we will reward you with good things for what you have done in our behalf. And we will remit to you many charges, and will give you gifts. And now I free you and all the Jews from tributes, and I release you from the customs of salt, and remit the crowns and the thirds of the seed. And the half of the fruit of trees, which is my share, I leave to you from this day forward, so that it shall not be taken of the land of Judea, and of the three cities that are added thereto out of Samaria and Galilee, from this day forth and for ever. And let Jerusalem be holy and free, with the borders thereof ,and let the tenths and tributes be for itself. I yield up also the power of the citadel that is in Jerusalem, and I give it to the high priest to place therein such men as he shall choose to keep it. And every soul of the Jews that has been carried captive from the land of Judea in all my kingdom, I set at liberty freely, that all be discharged from tributes even of their cattle. And I will that all the feasts, and the Sabbaths, and the new moons, and the days appointed, and three days before the solemn day, and three days after the solemn day, be all days of immunity and freedom, for all the Jews that are in my kingdom. And no

man shall have power to do any thing against them, or to molest any of them, in any cause. And let there be enrolled in the king's army to the number of thirty thousand of the Jews, and allowance shall be made them as is due to all the king's forces, and certain of them shall be appointed to be in the fortresses of the great king. And some of them shall be set over the affairs of the kingdom, that are of trust, and let the governors be taken from among themselves, and let them walk in their own laws, as the king has commanded in the land of Judea. And the three cities that are added to Judea, out of the country of Samaria, let them be accounted with Judea that they may be under one and obey no other authority but that of the high priest. Ptolemais, and the confines thereof, I give as a free gift to the holy places that are in Jerusalem, for the necessary charges of the holy things. And I give every year fifteen thousand sicles of silver out of the king's accounts, of what belongs to me. And all that is above, which they that were over the affairs the years before, had not paid, from this time they shall give it to the works of the house. Moreover the five thousand sicles of silver which they received from the account of the holy places, every year, shall also belong to the priests that execute the ministry. And whosoever shall flee into the Temple that is in Jerusalem, and in all the borders thereof, being indebted to the king for any matter, let them be set at liberty, and all that they have in my kingdom, let them have it free. For the building also, or repairing the works of the holy places, the charges shall be given out of the king's revenues. For the building also of the walls of Jerusalem, and the fortifying thereof round about, the charges shall be given out of the king's account, as also for the building of the walls in Judea.

Now when Jonathan and the people heard these words, they gave no credit to them nor received them, because they remembered the great evil that he had done in Israel, for he had afflicted them exceedingly. And their inclinations were towards Alexander, because he had been the chief promoter of peace in their regard, and him they always helped. And King Alexander gathered together a great army and moved his camp near to Demetrius. And the two kings joined battle, and the army of Demetrius fled away, and Alexander pursued after him and pressed them close. And the battle was hard fought till the sun went down, and Demetrius was slain that day.

Treaty of Ptolemy and Alexander.

Alexander sent ambassadors to Ptolemy king of Egypt with words to this effect, saying, "Forasmuch as I am returned into my kingdom, and am set in the throne of my ancestors and have gotten the dominion, and have overthrown Demetrius, and possessed our country, and have joined battle with him, and both he and his army have been destroyed by us, and we are placed in the throne of his kingdom. Now therefore let us make friendship one with another, and give me now your daughter to wife, and I will be your son in law, and I will give both you and her gifts worthy of you." And King Ptolemy answered, saying, "Happy is the day wherein you returned to the land of your fathers, and sat in the throne of their kingdom. And now I will do to you as you have written, but meet me at Ptolemais, that we may see one another, and I may give her to you as you have said." So Ptolemy went out of Egypt with Cleopatra his daughter, and he came to Ptolemais in the hundred and sixty-second year. King Alexander met him, and he gave him his daughter Cleopatra. And he celebrated her marriage at Ptolemais with great glory, after the manner of kings. King Alexander wrote to Jonathan, that he should come and meet him. And he went honorably to Ptolemais, and he met there the two kings, and he gave them much silver and gold and presents, and he found favor in their sight. And some pestilent men of Israel, men of a wicked life, assembled themselves against him to accuse him, but the king gave no heed to them. He commanded that Jonathan's garments should be taken off and that he should be clothed with purple, and they did so. And the king made him sit by himself. And he said to his princes, "Go out with him into the midst of the city and make proclamation that no man complain against him of any matter, and that no man trouble him for any manner of cause." So when his accusers saw his glory proclaimed, and him clothed with purple, they all fled away. And the king magnified him, and enrolled him amongst his chief friends, and made him governor and partaker of his dominion. And Jonathan returned into Jerusalem with peace and joy.

Jonathan Defeats Apollonius.

In the year one hundred and sixty-five Demetrius the son of Demetrius came from Crete into the land of his fathers. And King Alexander heard of it, and was much troubled, and returned to Antioch. And King Demetrius made Apollonius his general, who was governor of Celesyria, and he gathered together a great army and came to Jamnia. And he sent to Jonathan the high priest, saying, "You alone stand against us, and I am laughed at and reproached, because you show your power against us in the mountains. Now therefore if you trust in your forces, come down to us into the plain, and there let us try one another, for with me is the strength of war. Ask, and learn who I am, and the rest that help me, who also say that your foot cannot stand before our face, for your fathers have twice been put to flight in their own land. And now how will you be able to abide the horsemen, and so great an army in the plain, where there is no stone, nor rock, nor place to flee to?" Now when Jonathan heard the words of Apollonius, he was moved in his mind and he chose ten thousand men and went out of Jerusalem, and Simon his brother met him to help him. They pitched their tents near Joppe, but they shut him out of the city, because a garrison of Apollonius was in Joppe, and he laid siege to it. And they that were in the city being affrighted, opened the gates to him, so Jonathan took Joppe. Apollonius heard of it, and he took three thousand horsemen, and a great army. And he went to Azotus as one that was making a journey, and immediately he went forth into the plain because he had a great number of horsemen, and he trusted in them. And Jonathan followed after him to Azotus, and they joined battle. Apollonius left privately in the camp a thousand horsemen behind them. And Jonathan knew that there was an ambush behind him, and they surrounded his army and cast darts at the people from morning till evening. But the people stood still, as Jonathan had commanded them, and so their horses were fatigued. Then Simon drew forth his army and attacked the legion, for the horsemen were wearied, and they were discomfited by him and fled. And they that were scattered about the plain fled into Azotus and went into Bethdagon, their idol's temple, to save themselves. But Jonathan set fire to Azotus and the cities that were around it, and took the spoils of them and the temple of Dagon, and all them that were fled into it, he burnt with fire. So they that were slain by the sword, with them that were burnt, were almost eight thousand men. And Jonathan removed his army from there and camped against Ascalon, and they went out of the city to meet him with great honor. And Jonathan returned into Jerusalem with his people, having many spoils. And it came to pass when Alexander the king heard these words, that he honored Jonathan yet more. And he sent him a buckle of gold, as the custom is, to be given to such as are of the royal blood. And he gave him Accaron and all the borders thereof in possession.

Chapter 11

Alliance of Ptolemy and Demetrius II.

The king of Egypt gathered together an army, like the sand that lies upon the seashore, and many ships, and he sought to get the kingdom of Alexander by deceit and join it to his own kingdom. And he went out into Syria with peaceable words, and they opened to him the cities, and met him, for King Alexander had ordered them to go forth to meet him because he was his father in law. Now when Ptolemy entered into the cities, he put garrisons of soldiers in every city. And when he came near to Azotus, they shewed him the temple of Dagon that was burnt with fire, and Azotus, and the suburbs thereof that were destroyed, and the bodies that were cast abroad, and the graves of them that were slain in the battle, which they had made near the way. And they told the king that Jonathan had done these things, to make him odious, but the king held his peace. And Jonathan came to meet the king at Joppe with glory, and they saluted one another, and they lodged there. And Jonathan went with the king as far as the river called Eleutherus, and he returned into Jerusalem. And King Ptolemy got the dominion of the cities by the sea side, even to Seleucia, and he devised evil designs against Alexander. And he sent ambassadors to Demetrius, saying, "Come, let us make a league between us, and I will give you my daughter whom Alexander has, and you shall reign in the kingdom of your father. For I repent that I have given him my daughter, for he has sought to kill me." And he slandered him, because he coveted his kingdom. And he took away his daughter, and gave her to Demetrius, and alienated himself from Alexander, and his enmities were made manifest. And Ptolemy entered into Antioch, and set two crowns upon his head, that of Egypt, and that of Asia. Now King Alexander was in Cilicia at that time because they that were in those places had rebelled. When Alexander heard of it he came to give him battle. King Ptolemy brought forth his army and met him with a strong power, and put him to flight. Alexander fled into Arabia to be protected, and King Ptolemy was exalted. Zabdiel the Arabian took off Alexander's head, and sent it to Ptolemy. And King Ptolemy died the third day after, and they that were in the strongholds were destroyed by them that were within the camp. And Demetrius reigned in the hundred and sixty-seventh year.

Alliance of Jonathan and Demetrius II.

In those days Jonathan gathered together them that were in Judea, to take the citadel that was in Jerusalem, and they made many engines of war against it. Then some wicked men that hated their own nation went away to King Demetrius and told him that Jonathan was besieging the citadel. When he heard it, he was angry, and forthwith he came to Ptolemais, and wrote to Jonathan, that he should not besiege the citadel, but should come to him in haste, and speak to him. But when Jonathan heard this, he bade them besiege it still, and he chose some of the ancients of Israel, and of the priests, and put himself in danger. And he took gold, and silver, and raiment, and many other presents, and went to the king to Ptolemais, and he found favor in his sight. And certain wicked men of his nation made complaints against him. And the king treated him as his predecessor had done before, and he exalted him in the sight of all his friends. And he confirmed him in the high priesthood, and all the honors he had before, and he made him the chief of his friends. And Jonathan requested of the king that he would make Judea free from tribute, and the three governments, and Samaria, and the confines thereof, and he promised him three hundred talents. The king consented and wrote letters to Jonathan of all these things to this effect:

"King Demetrius to his brother Jonathan, and to the nation of the Jews, greeting. We send you here a copy of the letter, which we have written to Lasthenes our parent concerning you, that you might know it. 'King Demetrius to Lasthenes his parent, greeting. We have determined to do good to the nation of the Jews who are our friends, and keep the things that are just with us, for their good will which they bear towards us. We have ratified therefore unto them all the borders of Judea, and the three cities, Apherema, Lydda, and Ramatha, which are added to Judea, out of Samaria, and all their confines, to be set apart to all them that sacrifice in Jerusalem, instead of the payments which the king received of them every year, and for the fruits of the land, and of the trees. And as for other things that belonged to us of the tithes, and of the tributes, from this time we discharge them of them, the saltpans also, and the crowns that were presented to us. We give all to them, and nothing hereof shall be revoked from this time forth and for ever. Now therefore see that you make a copy of these things, and let it be given to Jonathan, and set upon the holy mountain, in a conspicuous place.'"

The Intrigue of Trypho.

And King Demetrius seeing that the land was quiet before him, and nothing resisted him, sent away all his forces, every man to his own place, except the foreign army, which he had drawn together from the islands of the nations, so all the troops of his fathers hated him. Now there was one Tryphon who had been of Alexander's party before, who seeing that all the army murmured against Demetrius, went to Emalchuel the Arabian, who brought up Antiochus the son of Alexander. And he pressed him much to deliver him to him, that he might be king in his father's place, and he told him all that Demetrius had done, and how his soldiers hated him. And he remained there many days.

Jonathan Aids Demetrius II.

And Jonathan sent to King Demetrius, desiring that he would cast out them that were in the citadel in Jerusalem, and those that were in the strongholds, because they fought against Israel. And Demetrius sent to Jonathan, saying, "I will not only do this for you, and for your people, but I will greatly honor you, and your nation, when opportunity shall serve. Now therefore you shall do well if you send me men to help me, for all my army is gone from me." And Jonathan sent him three thousand valiant men to Antioch, and they came to the king, and the king was very glad of their coming. And they that were of the city assembled themselves together, to the number of a hundred and twenty thousand men, and would have killed the king. And the king fled into the palace, and they of the city kept the passages of the city, and began to fight. And the king called the Jews to his assistance, and they came to him all at once, and they all dispersed themselves through the city. And they slew in that day a hundred thousand men, and they set fire to the city, and got many spoils that day, and delivered the king. And they that were of the city saw that the Jews had got the city as they would, and they were discouraged in their minds, and cried to the king, making supplication, and saying, "Grant us peace, and let the Jews cease from assaulting us, and the city." And they threw down their arms, and made peace, and the Jews were glorified in the sight of the king, and in the sight of all that were in his realm, and were renowned throughout the kingdom, and returned to Jerusalem with many spoils. So King Demetrius sat in the throne of his kingdom, and the land was quiet before him. And he falsified all whatsoever he had said, and alienated himself from Jonathan, and did not reward him according to the benefits he had received from him, but gave him great trouble.

Alliance of Jonathan and Antiochus VI.

And after this Tryphon returned, and with him Antiochus the young boy, who was made king, and put on the diadem. And there assembled unto him all the hands which Demetrius had sent away, and they fought against Demetrius, who turned his back and fled. And Tryphon took the elephants, and made himself master of Antioch. And young Antiochus wrote to Jonathan, saying, "I confirm you in the high priesthood, and I appoint you ruler over the four cities, and to be one of the king's friends." And he sent him vessels of gold for his service, and he gave him leave to drink in gold, and to be clothed in purple, and to wear a golden buckle. And he made his brother Simon governor from the borders of Tyre even to the confines of Egypt.

Campaigns of Jonathan and Simon.

Then Jonathan went forth and passed through the cities beyond the river, and all the forces of Syria gathered themselves to him to help him, and he came to Ascalon, and they met him honorably out of the city. And he went from there to Gaza, and they that were in Gaza shut him out, and he besieged it and burnt all the suburbs round about, and took the spoils. And the men of Gaza made supplication to Jonathan, and he gave them the right hand, and he took their sons for hostages, and sent them to Jerusalem, and he went through the country as far as Damascus. And Jonathan heard that the generals of Demetrius were come treacherously to Cades, which is in Galilee, with a great army, purposing to remove him from the affairs of the kingdom. And he went against them, but left his brother Simon in the country. And Simon encamped against Bethsura, and assaulted it many days, and shut them up. And they desired him to make peace, and he granted it them. And he cast them out from there, and took the city, and placed a garrison in it. And Jonathan and his army encamped by the water of Genesar, and before it was light they were ready in the plain of Asor. And behold the army of the strangers met him in the plain, and they laid an ambush for him in the mountains, but he went out against them. And they that lay in ambush arose out of their places, and joined battle. And all that were on Jonathan's side fled, and none was left of them, but Mathathias the son of Absalom, and Judah the son of Calphi, chief captain of the army. And Jonathan rent his garments, and cast earth upon his head, and prayed. And Jonathan turned again to them to battle, and he put them to flight, and they fought. And they of his part that fled saw this, and they turned again to him, and they all with him pursued the enemies even to Cades, to their own camp. And there fell of the aliens in that day three thousand men, and Jonathan returned to Jerusalem.

Chapter 12

Alliances with Rome and Sparta.

And Jonathan saw that the time served him, and he chose certain men and sent them to Rome, to confirm and to renew the amity with them. And he sent letters to the Spartans, and to other places according to the same form. And they went to Rome, and entered into the senate house, and said, "Jonathan the high priest and the nation of the Jews have sent us to renew the amity and alliance as it was before." And they gave them letters to their governors in every place, to conduct them into the land of Judea with peace. And this is a copy of the letters which Jonathan wrote to the Spartans:

> Jonathan the high priest, and the ancients of the nation, and the priests, and the rest of the people of the Jews, to the Spartans, their brethren, greeting. There were letters sent long ago to Onias the high priest from Arius who reigned then among you, to signify that you are our brethren, as the copy here underwritten does specify. And Onias received the ambassador with honor, and received the letters wherein there was mention made of the alliance, and amity. We, though we needed none of these things, having for our comfort the holy books that are in our hands, chose rather to send to you to renew the brotherhood and friendship, lest we should become strangers to you altogether, for there is a long time passed since you sent to us. We therefore at all times without ceasing, both in our festivals, and other days, wherein it is convenient, remember you in the sacrifices that we offer, and in our observances, as it is meet, and becoming to remember brethren. And we rejoice at your glory. But we have had many troubles and wars on every side, and the kings that are round about us have fought against us. But

we would not be troublesome to you, nor the rest of our allies and friends in these wars. For we have had help from heaven, and we have been delivered, and our enemies are humbled. We have chosen therefore Numenius the son of Antiochus, and Antipater the son of Jason, and have sent them to the Romans to renew with them the former amity and alliance. And we have commanded them to go also to you, and to salute you, and to deliver you our letters, concerning the renewing of our brotherhood. And now you shall do well to give us an answer hereto.

And this is the copy of the letter which he had sent to Onias:

Arius king of the Spartans to Onias the high priest, greeting. It is found in writing concerning the Spartans, and the Jews, that they are brethren, and that they are of the stock of Abraham. And now since this is come to our knowledge, you do well to write to us of your prosperity. And we also have written back to you that our cattle and possessions are yours, and yours, ours. We therefore have commanded that these things should be told you.

More Campaigns of Jonathan and Simon.

Now Jonathan heard that the generals of Demetrius were come again with a greater army than before to fight against him. So he went out from Jerusalem and met them in the land of Amath, for he gave them no time to enter into his country. And he sent spies into their camp, and they came back and brought him word that they designed to come upon them in the night. And when the sun was set, Jonathan commanded his men to watch, and to be in arms all night long ready to fight, and he set sentinels round about the camp. And the enemies heard that Jonathan and his men were ready for battle, and they were struck with fear, and dread in their heart, and they kindled fires in their camp. But Jonathan and they that were with him knew it not till the morning, for they saw the lights burning. And Jonathan pursued after them, but overtook them not, for they had passed the river Eleutherus. And Jonathan turned upon the Arabians that are called Zabadeans, and he defeated them and took the spoils. He went forward and came to Damascus, and passed through all that country. Simon also went forth, and came as far as Ascalon and the neighboring fortresses, and he turned aside to Joppe and took possession of it (for he heard that they designed to deliver the hold to them that took part with Demetrius), and he put a garrison there to keep it. And Jonathan came back and called together the ancients of the people, and he took a resolution with them to build fortresses in Judea, and to build up walls in Jerusalem, and raise a mount between the citadel and the city, to separate it from the city, that so it might have no communication, and that they might neither buy nor sell. And they came together to build up the city, for the wall that was upon the brook towards the east was broken down, and he repaired that which is called Caphetetha, and Simon built Adiada in Sephela, and fortified it, and set up gates and bars.

Capture of Jonathan.

Now when Tryphon had conceived a design to make himself king of Asia, and to take the crown, and to stretch out his hand against King Antiochus, fearing lest Jonathan would not suffer him, but would fight against him, he sought to seize upon him, and to kill him. So he rose up and came to Bethsan. And Jonathan went out to meet him with forty thousand men chosen for battle, and came to Bethsan. Now when Tryphon saw that Jonathan came with a great army, he dared not stretch forth his hand against him, but received him with honor and commended him to all his friends, and gave him presents, and he commanded his troops to obey him as himself. And he said to Jonathan, "Why have you troubled all the people, whereas we have no war? Now therefore send them back to their own houses and choose a few men that may be with you, and come with me to Ptolemais, and I will deliver it to you, and the rest of the strongholds, and the army, and all that have any charge, and I will return and go away, for this is the cause of my coming." And Jonathan believed him, and did as he said, and sent away his army, and they departed into the land of Judea. But he kept with him three thousand men of whom he sent two thousand into Galilee and one thousand went with him. Now as soon as Jonathan entered into Ptolemais, they of Ptolemais shut the gates of the city and took him, and all them that came in with him they slew with the sword. Then Tryphon sent an army and horsemen into Galilee, and into the great plain to destroy all Jonathan's company. But they, when they understood that Jonathan and all that were with him were taken and slain, encouraged one another, and went out ready for battle. Then they that had come after them, seeing that they stood for their lives, returned back. Whereupon they all came peaceably into the land of Judea. And they bewailed Jonathan and them that had been with him exceedingly, and Israel mourned with great lamentation. Then all the heathens that were round about them, sought to destroy them. For they said, "They have no prince, nor any to help them. Now therefore let us make war upon them, and take away the memory of them from amongst men."

Chapter 13

Simon as Leader.

Now Simon heard that Tryphon was gathering together a very great army, to invade the land of Judea and to destroy it. And seeing that the people were in dread, and in fear, he went up to Jerusalem and assembled the people, and exhorted them, saying, "You know what great battles I and my brethren, and the house of my father, have fought for the laws, and the sanctuary, and the distresses that we have seen. By reason whereof all my brethren have lost their lives for Israel's sake, and I am left alone. And now far be it from me to spare my life in any time of trouble, for I am not better than my brethren. I will avenge then my nation and the sanctuary, and our children and wives, for all the heathens are gathered together to destroy us out of mere malice." And the spirit of the people was kindled as soon as they heard these words. And they answered with a loud voice saying, "You are our leader in the place of Judah, and Jonathan your brother. Fight our battles, and we will do whatsoever you shall say to us." So gathering together all the men of war, he made haste to finish all the walls of Jerusalem, and he fortified it round about. And he sent Jonathan the son of Absalom, and with him a new army into Joppe, and he cast out them that were in it, and remained there.

Trypho's Deceit.

And Tryphon removed from Ptolemais with a great army, to invade the land of Judea, and Jonathan was with him in custody. But Simon pitched in Addus, over against the plain. And when Tryphon understood that Simon was risen up in the place of his brother Jonathan, and that he meant to join battle with him, he sent messengers to him, saying, "We have detained your brother Jonathan for the money that he owed in the king's account, by reason of the affairs which he had the management of. But now send a hundred talents of silver, and his two sons for hostages, that when he is set at liberty he may not revolt from us, and we will release him." Now Simon knew that he spoke deceitfully to him, nevertheless he ordered the money and the children to be sent, lest he should bring upon himself a great hatred of the people of Israel, who might have said, "Because he sent not the money, and the children, therefore is he lost." So he sent the children, and the hundred talents, but Tryphon lied and did not let Jonathan go. And after this Tryphon entered within the country to destroy it, and they went about by the way that leads to Ador, and Simon and his army marched to every place wherever they went. And they that were in the citadel sent messengers to Tryphon, that he should make haste to come through the desert, and send them provisions. And Tryphon made ready all his horsemen to come that night, but there fell a very great snow, and he came not into the country of Gilead. And when he approached to Bascama, he slew Jonathan and his sons there. And Tryphon returned, and went into his own country.

Jonathan's Tomb.

And Simon sent, and took the bones of Jonathan his brother and buried them in Modin, in the city of his fathers. And all Israel bewailed him with great lamentation, and they mourned for him many days. And Simon built over the sepulcher of his father and of his brethren, a building lofty to the sight, of polished stone behind and before. And he set up seven pyramids one against another for his father and his mother, and his four brethren. And round about these he set great pillars and upon the pillars arms for a perpetual memory, and by the arms ships carved, which might be seen by all that sailed on the sea. This is the sepulcher that he made in Modin even unto this day.

Alliance of Simon and Demetrius II.

But Tryphon when he was upon a journey with the young King Antiochus, treacherously slew him. And he reigned in his place, and put on the crown of Asia, and brought great evils upon the land. Simon built up the strongholds of Judea, fortifying them with high towers, great walls, gates and bars, and he stored up provisions in the fortresses. And Simon chose men and sent to King Demetrius, to the end that he should grant an immunity to the land, for all that Tryphon did was to spoil. And King Demetrius in answer to this request, wrote a letter in this manner:

> "King Demetrius to Simon the high priest, and friend of kings, and to the ancients, and to the nation of the Jews, greeting. The golden crown, and the palm, which you sent, we have received, and we are ready to make a firm peace with you, and to write to the king's chief officers to release you the things that we have released. For all that we have decreed in your favor shall stand in force. The strongholds that you have built shall be your own. And as for any oversight or fault committed unto this day, we forgive it, and the crown which you owed, and if any other thing were taxed in Jerusalem, now let it not be taxed. And if any of you be fit to be enrolled among ours, let them be enrolled, and let there be peace between us."

In the year one hundred and seventy the yoke of the Gentiles was taken off from Israel. And the people of Israel began to write in the instruments, and public records, "The first year under Simon the high priest, the great captain and prince of the Jews."

Simon Captures Gazara.

In those days Simon besieged Gaza and camped round about it, and he made engines and set them to the city, and he struck one tower, and took it. And they that were within the engine leaped into the city, and there was a great uproar. And they that were in the city went up with their wives and children upon the wall, with their garments rent, and they cried with a loud voice, beseeching Simon to grant them peace. And they said, "Deal not with us according to our evil deeds, but according to your mercy." And Simon being moved, did not destroy them, but yet he cast them out of the city, and cleansed the houses wherein there had been idols, and then he entered into it with hymns, blessing the Lord. And having cast out of it all uncleanness, he placed in it men that should observe the Torah, and he fortified it, and made it his habitation.

Simon Captures the Citadel.

But they that were in the citadel of Jerusalem were hindered from going out and coming into the country, and from buying and selling, and they were straitened with hunger, and many of them perished through famine. They cried to Simon for peace, and he granted it to them. He cast them out from there and cleansed the citadel from uncleannesses. And they entered into it the twenty-third day of the second month, in the year one hundred and seventy-one, with thanksgiving, and branches of palm trees, and harps, and cymbals, and psalteries, and hymns, and canticles, because the great enemy was destroyed out of Israel. And he ordained that these days should be kept every year with gladness. And he fortified the mountain of the Temple that was near the citadel, and he dwelt there himself, and they that were with him. And Simon saw that John his son was a valiant man for war, and he made him captain of all the forces, and he dwelt in Gazara.

CHAPTER 14

Capture of Demetrius II.

In the year one hundred and seventy-two, King Demetrius assembled his army and went into Media to get him succours to fight against Tryphon. And Arsaces the king of Persia and Media heard that Demetrius entered within his borders, and he sent one of his princes to take him alive, and bring him to him. And he went and defeated the army of Demetrius and took him, and brought him to Arsaces, and he put him into custody.

Praise of Simon

And all the land of Judea was at rest all the days of Simon, and he sought the good of his nation, and his power and glory pleased them well all his days. And with all his glory he took Joppe for a haven, and made an entrance to the isles of the sea. And he enlarged the bounds of his nation, and made himself master of the country. And he gathered together a great number of captives, and had the dominion of Gazara, and of Bethsura, and of the citadel, and took away all uncleanness out of it, and there was none that resisted him. Every man tilled his land with peace, and the land of Judea yielded her increase, and the trees of the fields their fruit. The ancient men sat all in the streets, and treated together of the good things of the land, and the young men put on them glory, and the robes of war. And he provided provisions for the cities, and he appointed that they should be furnished with ammunition, so that the fame of his glory was renowned even to the end of the earth. He made peace in the land, and Israel rejoiced with great joy. And every man sat under his vine, and under his fig tree, and there was none to make them afraid. There was none left in the land to fight against them; kings were discomfited in those days. And he strengthened all those of his people that were brought low, and he sought the Torah, and took away every unjust and wicked man. He glorified the sanctuary, and multiplied the vessels of the holy places.

Alliance with Rome and Sparta.

And it was heard at Rome, and as far as Sparta, that Jonathan was dead, and they were very sorry. But when they heard that Simon his brother was made high priest in his place, and was possessed of all the country, and the cities therein, they wrote to him in tables of brass, to renew the friendship and alliance which they had made with Judah, and with Jonathan his brethren. And they were read before the assembly in Jerusalem. And this is the copy of the letters that the Spartans sent:

> The princes and the cities of the Spartans to Simon the high priest, and to the ancients, and the priests, and the rest of the people of the Jews their brethren, greeting. The ambassadors that were sent to our people have told us of your glory, honor, and joy, and we rejoice at their coming. And we registered what was said by them in the councils of the people in this manner:

> Numenius the son of Antiochus, and Antipater the son of Jason, ambassadors of the Jews, came to us to renew the former friendship with us. And it pleased the people to receive the men honorably, and to put a copy of their words in the pub-

lic records, to be a memorial to the people of the Spartans. And we have written a copy of them to Simon the high priest.

And after this Simon sent Numenius to Rome with a great shield of gold, the weight of a thousand pounds, to confirm the league with them.

Official Honors for Simon.

And when the people of Rome had heard these words, they said, "What thanks shall we give to Simon and his sons? For he has restored his brethren, and has driven away in fight the enemies of Israel from them." And they decreed him liberty, and registered it in tables of brass, and set it upon pillars in Mount Zion. And this is a copy of the writing:

> The eighteenth day of the month Elul, in the year one hundred and seventy-two, being the third year under Simon the high priest at Asaramel, in a great assembly of the priests, and of the people, and the princes of the nation, and the ancients of the country, these things were notified. Forasmuch as there have often been wars in our country, and Simon the son of Mathathias of the children of Jarib, and his brethren have put themselves in danger, and have resisted the enemies of their nation, for the maintenance of their holy places, and the Torah, and have raised their nation to great glory. And Jonathan gathered together his nation, and was made their high priest, and he was laid to his people. And their enemies desired to tread down and destroy their country, and to stretch forth their hands against their holy places. Then Simon resisted and fought for his nation, and laid out much of his money, and armed the valiant men of his nation, and gave them wages. And he fortified the cities of Judea and Bethsura that lie in the borders of Judea, where the armor of the enemies was before, and he placed there a garrison of Jews. And he fortified Joppe which lies by the sea, and Gazara, which borders upon Azotus, wherein the enemies dwelt before, and he placed Jews here and furnished them with all things convenient for their reparation. And the people seeing the acts of Simon, and to what glory he meant to bring his nation, made him their prince, and high priest, because he had done all these things, and for the justice, and faith, which he kept to his nation, and for that he sought by all means to advance his people. And in his days things prospered in his hands, so that the heathens were taken away out of their country, and they also that were in the city of David in Jerusalem in the citadel, out of which they issued forth, and profaned all places round about the sanctuary, and did much evil to its purity. And he placed therein Jews for the defense of the country, and of the city, and he raised up the walls of Jerusalem. And King Demetrius confirmed him in the high priesthood. According to these things he made him his friend, and glorified him with

great glory. For he had heard that the Romans had called the Jews their friends, and confederates, and brethren, and that they had received Simon's ambassadors with honor, and that the Jews, and their priests, had consented that he should be their prince, and high priest for ever, till there should arise a faithful prophet. And that he should be chief over them, and that he should have the charge of the sanctuary, and that he should appoint rulers over their works, and over the country, and over the armor, and over the strongholds. And that he should have care of the holy places, and that he should be obeyed by all, and that all the writings in the country should be made in his name, and that he should be clothed with purple, and gold. And that it should not be lawful for any of the people, or of the priests, to disannul any of these things, or to gainsay his words, or to call together an assembly in the country without him, or to be clothed with purple, or to wear a buckle of gold. And whosoever shall do otherwise, or shall make void any of these things shall be punished. And it pleased all the people to establish Simon, and to do according to these words. And Simon accepted thereof, and was well pleased to execute the office of the high priesthood, and to be captain, and prince of the nation of the Jews, and of the priests, and to be chief over all.

And they commanded that this writing should be put in tables of brass, and that they should be set up within the compass of the sanctuary in a conspicuous place, and that a copy thereof should be put in the treasury, that Simon and his sons may have it.

Chapter 15

Letter of Antiochus VII.

And King Antiochus the son of Demetrius sent letters from the isles of the sea to Simon the priest, and prince of the nation of the Jews, and to all the people, and the contents were these:

King Antiochus to Simon the high priest, and to the nation of the Jews, greeting. Forasmuch as certain pestilent men have usurped the kingdom of our fathers, and my purpose is to challenge the kingdom and to restore it to its former estate, and I have chosen a great army, and have built ships of war. And I design to go through the country that I may take revenge of them that have destroyed our country, and that have made many cities desolate in my realm. Now therefore I confirm unto you all the oblations which all the kings before me remitted to you, and what other gifts soever they remitted to you. And I give you leave to coin your own money in your country. And let Jerusalem be holy and free, and all the armor that has been made, and the fortresses which you have built, and which you keep in your hands, let them remain to you. And all that is due to the king, and what should be the king's hereafter, from this present and for ever, is forgiven. And when we shall have recovered our kingdom, we will glorify you, and your nation, and the Temple with great glory, so that your glory shall be made manifest in all the earth.

In the year one hundred and seventy-four Antiochus entered into the land of his fathers, and all the forces assembled to him, so that few were left with Tryphon. And King Antiochus pursued after him, and he fled along by the sea coast and came to Dora, for he perceived that evils were gathered together upon him, and his troops had forsaken him. And Antiochus camped above Dora with a hundred and twenty thousand men of war, and eight thousand horsemen. And he invested the city, and the ships drew near by sea, and they annoyed the city by land and by sea, and suffered none to come in or go out.

Roman Alliance Renewed.

Numenius, and they that had been with him, came from the city of Rome, having letters written to the kings, and countries, the contents whereof were these:

> Lucius the consul of the Romans, to King Ptolemy, greeting. The ambassadors of the Jews our friends came to us, to renew the former friendship and alliance, being sent from Simon the high priest, and the people of the Jews. And they brought also a shield of gold of a thousand pounds. It has seemed good therefore to us to write to the kings, and countries, that they should do them no harm, nor fight against them, their cities, or countries, and that they should give no aid to them that fight against them. And it has seemed good to us to receive the shield of them. If therefore any pestilent men are fled out of their country to you, deliver them to Simon the high priest, that he may punish them according to their law.

These same things were written to King Demetrius, and to Attalus, and to Ariarathes, and to Arsaces, and to all the countries; and to Lampsacus, and to the Spartans, and to Delus, and Myndus, and Sicyon, and Caria, and Samus, and Pamphylia, and Lycia, and Alicarnassus, and Cos, and Side, and Aradus, and Rhodes, and Phaselis, and Gortyna, and Gnidus, and Cyprus, and Cyrene. And they wrote a copy thereof to Simon the high priest, and to the people of the Jews.

Hostility from Antiochus VII.

But King Antiochus moved his camp to Dora the second time, assaulting it continually, and making engines, and shut up Tryphon, that he could not go out. And Simon sent to him two thousand chosen men to aid him, silver also, and gold, and abundance of furniture. And he would not receive them, but broke all the covenant that he had made with him before, and alienated himself from him. And he sent to him Athenobius one of his friends, to treat with him, saying:

> You hold Joppe, and Gazara, and the citadel that is in Jerusalem, which are cities of my kingdom. Their borders you have wasted, and you have made great havoc in the land, and have got the dominion of many places in my kingdom. Now therefore deliver up the cities that you have taken, and the tributes of the places whereof you have gotten the dominion without the borders of Judea. But if not, give me for them five hundred talents of silver, and for the havoc that you have made, and the tributes of the cities other five hundred talents, or else we will come and fight against you.

So Athenobius, the king's friend, came to Jerusalem and saw the glory of Simon and his magnificence in gold, and silver, and his great equipage, and he was astonished, and told him the king's words. And Simon answered him, and said to him, "We have neither taken other men's land, neither do we hold that which is other men's, but the inheritance of our fathers, which was for some time unjustly possessed by our enemies. But we having opportunity claim the inheritance of our fathers. And as to your complaints concerning Joppe and Gazara, they did great harm to the people, and to our country, yet for these we will give a hundred talents." And Athenobius answered him not a word. But returning in a rage to the king, made report to him of these words, and of the glory of Simon, and of all that he had seen, and the king was exceedingly angry.

Victory over Cendebeus.

And Tryphon fled away by ship to Orthosias. And the king appointed Cendebeus captain of the sea coast, and gave him an army of footmen and horsemen. And he commanded him to march with his army towards Judea, and he commanded him to build up Gedor, and to fortify the gates of the city, and to war against the people. But the king himself pursued after Tryphon. And Cendebeus came to Jamnia and began to provoke the people, and to ravage Judea, and to take the people prisoners, and to kill, and to build Gedor. And he placed there horsemen, and an army, that they might issue forth and make incursions upon the ways of Judea, as the king had commanded him.

Chapter 16

Then John came up from Gazara, and told Simon his father what Cendebeus had done against their people. And Simon called his two eldest sons, Judah and John, and said to them:

> I and my brethren, and my father's house, have fought against the enemies of Israel from our youth even to this day, and things have prospered so well in our hands that we have delivered Israel oftentimes. And now I am old, but be you instead of me, and my brethren, and go out, and fight for our nation, and the help from heaven be with you.

Then he chose out of the country twenty thousand fighting men, and horsemen, and they went forth against Cendebeus and rested in Modin. And they arose in the morning and went into the plain, and behold a very great army of footmen and horsemen came against them, and there was a running river between them. And he and his people pitched their camp over against them, and he saw that the people were afraid to go over the river, so he went over first. Then the men seeing him, passed over after him. And he divided the people, and set the horsemen in the midst of the footmen, but the horsemen of the enemies were very numerous. They sounded the holy trumpets, and Cendebeus and his army were put to flight, and there fell many of them wounded, and the rest fled into the stronghold. At that time Judah, John's brother, was wounded, but John pursued after them till he came to Cedron, which he had built. And they fled even to the towers that were in the fields of Azotus, and he burnt them with fire. And there fell of them two thousand men, and he returned to Judea in peace.

Murder of Simon and His Sons.

Now Ptolemy the son of Abobus was appointed captain in the plain of Jericho, and he had abundance of silver and gold, for he was son in law of the high priest. And his heart was lifted up, and he designed to make himself master of the country, and he purposed treachery against Simon, and his sons, to destroy them. Now Simon, as he was going through the cities that were in the country of Judea, and taking care for the good ordering of them, went down to Jericho, he and Mathathias and Judah his sons, in the year one hundred and seventy-seven, the eleventh month, the same is the month Sabath. And the son of Abobus received them deceitfully into a little fortress that is called Doch, which he had built, and he made them a great feast, and hid men there. And when Simon and his sons had drunk plentifully, Ptolemy and his men rose up and took their weapons, and entered into the banqueting place, and slew him, and his two sons, and some of his servants. And he committed a great treachery in Israel, and rendered evil for good. And Ptolemy wrote these things and sent to the king that he should send him an army to aid him, and he would deliver him the country, and their cities, and tributes. And he sent others to Gazara to kill John. And to the tribunes he sent letters to come to him, and that he would give them silver, and gold, and gifts. And he sent others to take Jerusalem, and the mountain of the Temple. Now one running before, told John in Gazara, that his father and his brethren were slain, and that he had sent men to kill him also. But when he heard it he was exceedingly afraid, and he apprehended the men that came to kill him and put them to death, for he knew that they sought to take him away. And as concerning the rest of the acts of John, and his wars, and the worthy deeds, which he bravely achieved, and the building of the walls, which he made, and the things that he did, behold these are written in the book of the days of his priesthood, from the time he was made high priest after his father.

Made in the USA
Las Vegas, NV
24 October 2022

57944545R00059